RIMSKY-KORSAKOV

AMS PRESS
NEW YORK

RIMSKY-KORSAKOV

A Short Biography

by

GERALD ABRAHAM

DUCKWORTH
3 HENRIETTA STREET
LONDON   W.C.2

Library of Congress Cataloging in Publication Data

Abraham, Gerald Ernest Heal, 1904-
    Rimsky-Korsakov: a short biography.

    Reprint of the 1945 ed. published by Duckworth,
London.
    Bibliography: p.
    1. Rimskiĭ-Korsakov, Nikolaĭ Andreevich, 1844-1908.
2. Composers—Russia—Biography.
ML410.R52A62   1976   780'.92'4 [B]   75-41002
ISBN 0-404-14500-0

Reprinted from an original copy in the collections
of the Newark Public Library

From the edition of 1945, London
First AMS edition published in 1976
Manufactured in the United States of America

AMS PRESS INC.
NEW YORK, N. Y.

CONTENTS

5

CHRONOLOGY

1844....Born at Tikhvin (Novgorod Government) (March 6th/18th).[1]

1856–62.At the Naval College, St. Petersburg.

1861....Meets Balakirev; begins First Symphony.

1862–65.Service in the *Almaz*.

1865....Symphony No. 1 in E flat minor performed (December 19th/31st).

1867....*Sadko* (musical picture) performed (December 9th/21st).

1869....*Antar* performed (March 10th/22nd).

1871....Appointed Professor of Practical Composition at the St. Petersburg Conservatoire.

1872....Marriage to Nadezhda Purgold (June 30th/July 12th).

1873....*Maid of Pskov* produced (January 1st/13th).

1873–75.Period of self-education.

1873–84.Inspector of Naval Bands.

1874....Début as conductor and first performance of Symphony No. 3 in C (February 18th/March 2nd).

1874–81.Director of Free School of Music.

1880....*May Night* produced (January 9th/21st).

1882....*Snow Maiden* produced (January 29th/February 10th); meeting with Belaev.

1883–94.Assistant Music Director of the Imperial Chapel.

[1] The first date in each case is the Russian one, 'old style'; the second is the equivalent according to the Western calendar.

1887....*Spanish Capriccio* performed (December
        5th/17th).

1888....*Sheherazade* and *Easter Festival* performed
        (December 3rd/15th).

1891–93.Period of physical and intellectual crisis,
        and distaste for music.

1892....*Mlada* produced (October 20th/November 1st).

1895....*Christmas Eve* produced (November 21st/
        December 3rd).

1897....*Sadko* (opera) produced (December 26th/
        January 7th, 1898).

1899....*The Tsar's Bride* produced (October
        22nd/November 3rd).

1900....*Tsar Saltan* produced (October 21st/
        November 2nd).

1905....Temporarily dismissed from the Peters-
        burg Conservatoire owing to political
        disturbances.

1907....*Kitezh* produced (February 7th/20th).

1908....Dies at Lyubensk (June 8th/21st).

1909....*The Golden Cockerel* produced (September
        24th/October 7th).

INTRODUCTION

'ALWAYS even-tempered, precise (what he said, he always did), serious, businesslike, simple and considerate, in the highest degree honourable, straightforward and self-controlled, incredibly industrious and conscientious—he could not fail to prepossess anyone who had the slightest contact with him. . . .' So Rimsky-Korsakov's character was summed up by one of his publishers, V. V. Bessel, a man who had not only had business relations with him for thirty years but had grown to know him as a friend. It is a summing-up with which no one who knows the evidence will disagree, and yet—surely—it leaves out something. That was the Rimsky-Korsakov who was seen by his publishers, his colleagues, his pupils; but it was not the orchestral wizard of *Sheherazade*, the lyric poet of *Snow Maiden*, the fairy-tale illustrator of *Tsar Saltan*, the Christian pantheist of *Kitezh*.

As readers of the following pages will discover, no one was more acutely conscious of this opposition between his art and his life than Rimsky-Korsakov himself. And it is recollection of this opposition which gives the story of his life much of its interest. Not that that life itself was wholly without fantasy; there can be few pages in musical history more fantastic than the one which tells how a serving officer in the Imperial Russian

Navy, ignorant of the very rudiments of musical theory, was appointed Professor of Composition in the St. Petersburg Conservatoire—and, incidentally, continued for some time to serve as a naval officer. Conversely, a certain amount of the man's own dry matter-of-factness was spilled over into his art and salts some of his most fantastic works with delicious irony. But whereas the man and the artist were almost inseparable in Tchaïkovsky—at least, in the mature Tchaïkovsky—they were almost completely separated in Rimsky-Korsakov.

These two composers had one quality in common, however: remarkable industry. The tale of Rimsky-Korsakov's labours—his own compositions and his work on his friends'—will be found at the end of the book in a list which is, I trust, fuller and more accurate than any previously published.

CHAPTER I

1844–61

Ancestry – birth – Uncle Pipon – first music-lessons – attempts at composition – enters Corps of Naval Cadets – musical experiences in Petersburg – relations with brother – studies with F. A. Canille – conducts a cadet choir.

IT was Rimsky-Korsakov's own opinion that he owed a great deal to his grandmothers. They were certainly intruders in such a distinguished family, though intruders of a kind not so very unusual in aristocratic Russian families in the good old days of feudalism and serfdom. It appears that Lieutenant-General Peter Voinovich Rimsky-Korsakov, son of one of the Empress Elisabeth's pet admirals, abducted a priest's daughter, who bore him five sons. Thanks to his influence, he was able to get them legitimized, and it was the third son, Andrey, Civil Governor of the Volïnsky Government from 1831 to 1835 and for a time a leading Freemason, who was to become the father of the composer. He was a simple, kind-hearted man with no idea of how to look after money. Very devout in his later years, he voluntarily freed his serfs long before the ukase of 1861. Andrey's first wife, Princess Meshchersky, having borne him no children, he married in 1821 the illegitimate, but fairly well-educated daughter of a wealthy landowner, a girl of nineteen. Her mother, too, had been a peasant, indeed a serf, and it pleased the composer to fancy he derived his love of folk-song

13

from the one grandmother, and his delight in religious rites and ceremonies from the other. At any rate the composer's mother, a beautiful, intelligent and devout woman, was thoroughly musical by nature; her son's collection of folksongs contains four melodies which he learned from her lips.[1]

Andrey's married life with this girl eighteen years younger than himself was ideally happy. But for many years she bore him only one child. The elder son, Voin, who entered the navy and died a rear-admiral in 1871, was born in 1822, the year after their marriage. But Andrey had been living in retirement at Tikhvin in the Novgorod Government for nine years before his wife gave him a second child on March 6th/18th, 1844. So it came about that Nicholas Andreevich Rimsky-Korsakov had a father of sixty, a mother of forty-two, and an only brother twenty-two years older than himself. The fifth member of the family at Tikhvin was Andrey's elder brother Peter, 'Uncle Pipon', an eccentric with the heart and mind of a child who, according to his grand-nephew, was 'a sort of Dickensian original of the type of Mr. Dick', his endless topic of conversation with himself being the arrival or non-arrival of the post. But 'Uncle Pipon' had two other passions: he loved the songs of the peasants and he worshipped devoutly at the great Monastery of the Blessed Virgin which faced the Rimsky-Korsakovs' house across the river. He, too, was laid under contribution when his nephew

[1] Mussorgsky introduced one of them in the inn scene of *Boris* as the drunken Varlaam's second song.

was collecting the old songs and we are indebted
to 'Uncle Pipon' for some of the loveliest tunes
in Russian music. His nephew's *Maid of Pskov*
and *Tsar Saltan*, and Balakirev's C major Symphony all owe some of their material to poor
cracked 'Uncle Pipon'.

That Monastery, too, left indelible impressions
on the small boy. He loved the singing of the
monks, particularly when they sang the music of
Bortnyansky. Many years later he recorded the
sound of the Monastery bells in his *Easter Overture*,
while the cry of the herald in *Snow Maiden* is a
recollection of the call of the mounted messenger
sent from the Monastery each summer to summon
the women of the place to help the monks with
their haymaking: 'Little aunts, little mothers,
pretty maidens, please come and rake hay for the
Mother of God'. There was a good deal of
music-making of a rather amateurish kind in the
home, in addition to the folk-songs of the boy's
mother and uncle; for the father, too, was musical
in his way, playing things like the romance from
Méhul's *Joseph*, 'Di tanti palpiti' from *Tancredi*,
the funeral march from *La Vestale*, and 'Ein
Mädchen oder Weibchen' from *The Magic Flute*
by ear on their old piano. But the mother's
influence seems to have been at least equally
important, though she was no longer a pianist.
(From her, incidentally, her son inherited a
curious tendency to take all music far too slowly.)
'The first signs of musical ability showed themselves in me very early', Rimsky-Korsakov tells
us in his memoirs. 'Before I was two I could
distinguish all the melodies my mother sang to

me; at three or four I was an expert at beating time on a drum to my father's piano-playing.[1] Father often purposely changed the time and rhythm suddenly, and I always followed him. I soon began to sing very accurately everything he played, and often sang with him; then I began to pick out the pieces with the harmonies for myself on the piano; and, having learned the names of the notes, would stand in another room and call them out when they were struck'.

At six he had his first regular lessons from an old lady, a neighbour. But he was unable to remember afterwards whether or not she was a good teacher, only that he was a bad pupil. 'I played inaccurately and was weak at counting'. On the whole he was better at reading and arithmetic than music, for which his liking was still very lukewarm. After a year or two the old lady's place as music-teacher was taken by a young governess, and hers in turn by a neighbour's daughter. Through them he first made the acquaintance of Beethoven, but most of the pieces he learned were easy fantasias on opera-melodies, *Les Huguenots*, *Le Prophète*, *Rigoletto*, *Zar und Zimmermann* and their kind. He also played duets with his teachers. But there was no amateur violinist or 'cellist in Tikhvin; even the local dance-band consisted only of one violin and one tambourine; so concerted music of every non-pianistic kind remained quite unknown to the

[1] Judging from one of the boy's letters home when a thirteen-year-old cadet, one of his father's favourite melodies was a tune the title of which the son spells in Roman characters: 'God saw Quine'. Perhaps the Crimean War had drawn attention to the enemy's national anthem.

child. He always insisted that 'generally speaking I was not an impressionable boy'. But it is not without significance that of all this music, other than that heard at the Monastery where the gorgeous ceremonial greatly deepened the impression, the pieces which gave him the greatest pleasure were Vanya's song and the duet from *A Life for the Tsar*, of which he found a copy at home. The duet seems to have provoked him to try to write one of his own, while another of his first, quite secret, attempts at composition took the form of an 'overture' for piano, a work of original design, beginning *adagio*, then quickening through an *andante*, a *moderato*, an *allegretto* and an *allegro* to a final *presto*.

He was twelve, and, except for a visit to his uncle, Admiral Nicholas Rimsky-Korsakov, in Petersburg, he had left the town of Tikhvin only three times in his life on short visits to friends in the country. He was a normal, healthy boy, climbing trees and so on; though, as a lonely child, compelled to invent most of his own amusements, playing coach-and-horses with chairs and making up conversations with himself as if between the driver and his passengers. But all the time he was obsessed by one dominant idea—to be a sailor. From 1852 to 1857 his brother was cruising [1] in the Far East, and Voin's letters home excited 'Niki's' imagination beyond measure. He devoured books about the sea, on which he had not yet set eyes, filled his head with nautical terms, and rigged up a model brig. Considering

[1] Part of the voyage is described by the novelist Goncharov in his travel-book, *The Frigate 'Pallada'*.

B

the number of sailors in the family it was natural enough that he, too, should enter the Imperial Navy. But the chief opposition came from Voin himself who, although he loved his profession, had a very poor opinion of his brother officers. 'Of the five or six hundred officers of the Baltic Fleet barely ten or fifteen love the service for its own sake', he wrote. 'A young fellow entering the Navy with poetic dreams in his head and hopes in his heart is quickly and bitterly disenchanted'. The general atmosphere of slackness was appalling. But 'Niki' was not to be discouraged. Nor could his father afford to enter him in the more aristocratic Corps of Pages. So at the end of July, 1856, Nicholas left his mother for the first time in his life and was taken by his father to Petersburg to enter the Corps of Naval Cadets, donning a uniform strongly suggestive of that fabulous English force, the Horse Marines.

Nicholas seems to have made a good cadet and to have been popular with his comrades, though he evidently found the discipline irksome at first. Not that he complained. But his letters home reveal an unconfessed homesickness. For the rest they are very boyish letters full of inquiries about his canaries, little reminiscences of home-life, Papa's piano-playing and so on. Forty years later he clearly remembered the anguish of his return to Petersburg from Tikhvin after the first summer holidays. There was a falling-off in his good behaviour, too. As for music, he had piano lessons for two years from one Ulich, a mediocre 'cellist and worse pianist, but took no interest in them. Nor was he taught the names of even the simplest chords and intervals. But he was allowed to spend each week-end with the Golovins, friends of his brother's, who were fond of Italian opera, particularly Rossini. Among other things they took him to hear *Lucia* 'which made a great impression on me'. After that came *Freischütz* and other operatic classics, many of them now dead and buried (of which *Robert le Diable* particularly delighted him by the sense of mystery in its orchestral colouring), and then—*A Life for the Tsar* which 'completely enraptured' him. At the same time he found at the Golovins' some separate numbers of *Ruslan*, the first music which awakened in him a sense of *harmonic* beauty. Besides, whereas genuine piano music was 'so dry and boring', 'when you play an opera', he wrote home, 'you imagine you're sitting in the theatre, listening or even playing or singing yourself; you imagine the scenery. In fact, it's frightfully jolly'. [1]

In the season of 1859–60 came a new revelation through the symphony concerts in the Grand Theatre. A couple of Beethoven symphonies and the *Midsummer Night's Dream* Overture aroused his enthusiasm, but Glinka's *Jota arragonesa* 'simply dazzled me'. He also heard *Ruslan* at the Maryinsky Theatre, and started buying the separate numbers with his pocket-money till Voin gave him the complete piano score, which had only just come out. *A Life for the Tsar* was also bought from his own limited funds. (According to his brother he had not the least sense of money

[1] A literal translation of his boyish slang, by the way; not a free, modernized equivalent.

—a trait inherited from his father.) Though his brother and the Golovins adopted a rather patronizing attitude towards Glinka, the recently dead master became his idol. He began to make all sorts of arrangements of Glinka's music for piano duet, piano and violin, piano and 'cello (without the slightest knowledge of the instruments) and even tried to orchestrate the entr'actes in *A Life for the Tsar* from the piano score. ' Naturally the devil only knows how it turned out! Seeing that it wouldn't do at all, I went twice to the publisher's shop and asked to see the orchestral score. I only half understood it, but the Italian names of the instruments, the terms *col* and *come sopra*, the different clefs and the transpositions of the horns and other instruments—all this exercised on me a certain mysterious charm. In short, I was a sixteen-year-old *child*, passionately fond of music *and playing with it*'. But according to his brother, who took a keen interest in his musical education, as in everything else he did, and supervised his piano practice, he still played even his favourite compositions very carelessly.

On his return home in 1857, Voin Rimsky-Korsakov had been appointed to the command of the gunnery instruction ship *Prokhor* and for two summers 'Niki' spent some time on board her with his brother. In June, 1858, he badly frightened Voin by falling out of the rigging into the sea, though without any serious consequences. The two brothers were devoted to each other, though, owing to the difference in their ages, Voin's relation to his younger brother was almost paternal. And fond of him as he was, he was too strict a disciplinarian to spoil him. Yet, in the summer and autumn of 1859, we find both of them, the boy of fifteen and the man of thirty-seven, in love with the same girl (a certain L. P. D——), and it is delightful to read in the elder brother's reports to their parents of his wise and careful handling of Niki's calf-love, his amused delight in the boy's little gallantries, and his taking advantage of the affair to make Niki smarten himself and improve his French. In January, 1862, before Nicholas had left the Naval College, Voin was appointed its Director, somewhat to the perturbation of their father, who feared, quite needlessly, that the situation might be bad for discipline. It was one of the old man's last thoughts, for he died the following month and his widow and Uncle Pipon moved to St. Petersburg to live with Voin.

In the meantime the dull and incompetent Ulich had been replaced in the autumn of 1859 [1] by a much more capable teacher, F. A. Canille, the first really good pianist the boy ever heard. 'I like Canille very much', his pupil wrote home. 'He makes the lesson interesting and not dry'. Not only that but he discovered that Canille shared his admiration of Glinka, considering him 'a great genius' and *Ruslan* 'the best opera in the world'. In the spring of 1860, we find Niki writing that 'I haven't been to the theatre as they've been giving nothing but things like *Il Trovatore* and *Traviata*—my musical ear doesn't care for that sort of trash; *we* love Glinka, Mendelssohn, Beethoven, Schumann, Chopin,

---

[1] Not 1860, as Rimsky-Korsakov says in his memoirs.

Meyerbeer and, perhaps, Rossini. Oh! and I'm
forgetting Fr. Schubert. . . .' Canille took a
keen interest in the sixteen-year-old cadet and
not only introduced him to Bach's fugues,
Balakirev's *King Lear* Overture, and other fresh
music, but encouraged him to compose, making
him ape early Beethoven in a sonata movement
and Glinka in a set of variations. He also gavè
him chorale melodies to harmonize and explained
some of the mysteries of an orchestral score to him,
but all in a very confused and unsystematic way;
so that the boy learned very little of even the
most elementary things. After a year Voin
decided that the lessons must end and Nicholas,
bitterly disappointed, had to obey. But Canille
invited the boy to visit him on Sundays, not for
regular lessons, but to talk about music and play
duets. Still knowing nothing, he says, of the
most elementary laws of part-writing—in spite
of his chorale exercises—or the names of chords,
much less of counterpoint, he concocted with
Canille's help two or three little piano pieces,
'watery rehashes of Glinka, Beethoven and
Schumann'. Among other musical activities at
this time we find Rimsky-Korsakov organizing
a choir of eighteen fellow-cadets and conducting
them in choruses from *A Life for the Tsar* and other
operas. But the authorities disapproved for some
reason and the choir had to disband.

CHAPTER II

1861–65

NOVEMBER 26th/December 8th, 1861, was a
memorable date in Rimsky-Korsakov's life, even
in the history of Russian music. ' Last Sunday',
he wrote to his parents, 'Canille introduced me to
M. A. Balakirev, a well-known musician and
composer, and also to Cui, who has written an
opera, *The Prisoner of the Caucasus*'. And a month
or two later: 'Yesterday I was at Balakirev's as
usual. I spend the time there so pleasantly that
I simply don't know how to thank Canille for such
a magnificent acquaintance'. He had at once
succumbed to the magnetism of Balakirev's
personality. At the very first meeting Balakirev
was shown the 'watery' piano pieces and 'a sort
of beginning of a Symphony in E flat minor'—incredible key, almost worthy of a popular novelist.
He approved of one of the pieces, a Scherzo in
C minor, and insisted that the lad should go on
with the Symphony. The twenty-two-year-old
Mussorgsky was there, too, also struggling to
write a symphony with very little better equip-
ment. But even he was transfigured in Rimsky-
Korsakov's eyes by the glamour of having had a
couple of compositions performed in public.

The seventeen-year-old cadet felt that he had fallen among real musicians at last. He was fascinated by their 'shop-talk' and by the wide culture of the critic V. V. Stassov, and he paid the greatest respect to their likes and dislikes. In after years he contended that he had weakly echoed their opinions, but it is clear that in many respects their tastes harmonized with those he had already formed. They liked Glinka and Schumann above all, admired the *Midsummer Night's Dream* Overture, disliked what they knew of Liszt and Wagner. So did he. In other respects he may have taken the colour of his surroundings, but it was a little ungenerous of him in later years to blame the twenty-four-year-old Balakirev for his own rather narrow taste at this period. Actually, it was Balakirev who first opened his eyes to much in the world of culture outside music—to history, literature and criticism. The Naval College had not even taught him to spell properly, much less history or anything of literature off the high road of the Russian classics: Pushkin, Lermontov, Gogol.

If Rimsky-Korsakov was overpowered by Balakirev's personality, Balakirev in turn took the strongest fancy to his new friend. He needed a 'pupil' of some sort. Gussakovsky, his chief hope, was abroad. He had a poor opinion of Mussorgsky's ability. But on Rimsky-Korsakov he built the most glowing expectations. 'I put my trust in you', he wrote a little later, 'as an old aunt in a young lawyer nephew'. Absurd as it seems, he at once set him—this boy with his appalling ignorance, knowing nothing of such mysteries as 'cadences'—to work at the already begun Symphony in E flat minor, and the first movement was finished within a month, during the Christmas holidays. With Balakirev's help Korsakov began to orchestrate it, and they all thought he showed a special aptitude for instrumentation. In the first few months of 1862, under Balakirev's close supervision, he wrote the scherzo (without a trio) and finale, composing the chief theme of the latter on the way back to Petersburg after his father's funeral, in March. But the Symphony, 'the first symphony ever written by a Russian' as Cui pointed out—maliciously denying Rubinstein's claim to Russianness—was destined to interruption. On April 8th/20th, 1862, the first of Russian symphonists left the Naval College as a *gardemarine* (neither cadet nor full-blown officer) and was appointed to the clipper *Almaz*.

Now the *Almaz* was being fitted out for a two or three years' cruise in foreign waters, and Rimsky-Korsakov was in despair at the prospect of leaving his new circle of friends, for he had just discovered that he wanted to be a musician and not a sailor. And Balakirev was most anxious not to lose him. But Cui, himself a serving officer, thought the lad should stay in the service, and Voin's robust common sense decided the matter; he saw no evidence that his brother was anything more than an intelligent amateur; Nicholas had a career before him in another sphere and there must be no spoiling it for the sake of a whim. As Nicholas agreed later in life, 'he was a thousand times right in considering me a dilettante, for that is all I was'. Even as a pianist, he was still very mediocre, a fair reader but with no technique.

In May, when Balakirev went to the Caucasus for the mineral waters and the other members of the circle and his relations also left Petersburg for the summer, Rimsky-Korsakov was left kicking his heels about in Kronstadt, and the symphony (which he had been trying to orchestrate with one eye on Berlioz's *Traité de l'Instrumentation* and the other on Glinka's scores) came to a full stop. Even with Balakirev at his elbow, his attempts to write a slow movement had failed. Generally speaking, Balakirev disapproved of sustained, 'singing' melody, considering it usually rather banal. And Rimsky-Korsakov found it was almost impossible to write slow music without lapsing into such *cantabile* melody. So during the summer he abandoned himself to the anything but intellectual society of his service-comrades. Three or four months passed in idleness, boredom and playing the fool generally. Balakirev came back and once more tried unsuccessfully to stop his sailing. But one day in late autumn he, Cui and Canille had to wave good-bye to their young friend from the steamer-jetty at Petersburg as he left to join his ship at Kronstadt. Two days later, October 21st/November 2nd, she sailed.

The *Almaz* made first for England, spending nearly four months at Gravesend for re-rigging. With the three other *gardemarines*, Rimsky-Korsakov made two sight-seeing expeditions to London, visiting Westminster Abbey, the Tower, the Crystal Palace and the rest of the sights. He also went to the Royal Italian Opera at Covent Garden, but forgot in after years what he had heard there. Having few duties, the *gardemarines* spent their leisure in discussing politics. There was a good library on board and one of the *gardemarines* bought a lot of French and English books—Buckle, Macaulay and John Stuart Mill. And they read Herzen's famous Socialist weekly, *The Bell*, banned in Russia, which he was then publishing in London. In religion and politics Rimsky-Korsakov was a typical young Russian liberal rationalist of the sixties, the 'age of reform'. Nor did he neglect music altogether, in spite of the obvious difficulties. He corresponded with Balakirev, who urged him to write the slow movement of his Symphony; and he obediently set to work, basing the movement on a folk-song given him by Balakirev, and posted the score home. (In accordance with some idea of Balakirev's, the *andante* was placed third, instead of second as in almost all classical symphonies.) 'I wrote it without the help of a piano (we hadn't one on board)', though they bought a harmonium in London, 'but once or twice at a public-house on shore I managed to play through what I had written'. One wonders in which of Gravesend's hotels or public-houses the first performance of part of the first Russian symphony was given by its composer.

Leaving England, the *Almaz* was ordered back to the Baltic to stop gun-running for the Polish rebels, with whom Korsakov and some of his comrades secretly sympathized. In the summer

she returned for a short time to Kronstadt and
Rimsky-Korsakov was able to spend three or four
days' leave in Petersburg, though his family and
musical friends were all in the country. But war
with England was believed to be imminent, owing
to the Polish insurrection, and the *Almaz* was
secretly despatched to New York in readiness to
act as a commerce-raider. Using her sails to
save her coal, and taking an unusual route to the
north of Scotland, she spent more than two
months over the voyage. With the rest of the
Russian squadron collected in American waters,
the *Almaz* remained from October, 1863, to
April, 1864, in the neighbourhood of New York,
Baltimore and Annapolis, the officers and *gardemarines* making excursions to the Chesapeake
Falls, to Washington and to Niagara, and spending
a good deal of time on shore with drink and
women. In New York Korsakov heard *Robert le
Diable* and Gounod's *Faust* badly performed, but
his own music-making was limited to vamping
accompaniments on the cabin harmonium to
American airs played on the fiddle by the pilot,
Thompson. The correspondence with Balakirev
nearly petered out. Korsakov had gradually
given up all thought of becoming a serious
musician; his one ambition now was to see the
world. Yet, quiet and timid by nature, he was
by no means shaping into a good officer. As he
admitted afterwards, he had 'no presence of mind
or administrative ability'. He was quite unable,
he says, to shout and bully in the approved style.
(His voice was nasal and rather shrill). To see a
sailor given two or three hundred stripes simply

revolted him. He was certainly not going to be an ornament to the Imperial Navy.

The danger of war with England being over, the *Almaz* was ordered home by way of Cape Horn and the Pacific, to the joy of Gardemarine Rimsky-Korsakov and disgust of Captain Zeleny. While his junior was delighting in the marvellous tropical nights, watching the phosphorescent water and the stars—which had always held a special fascination for him—the good Captain seems to have been exercising his ingenuity to avoid the Pacific crossing. Having taken sixty-five days to reach Rio de Janeiro from New York under sail, he decided to continue under steam; broke down his engines; returned to Rio for repairs; sent home a highly-coloured report of the vessel's unseaworthiness; and stayed at Rio till October, waiting for instructions. He was rewarded by orders to return to Europe, and in December, 1864, the *Almaz* rejoined Lesovsky's squadron in the Gulf of Villa Franca. Rimsky-Korsakov saw something of Nice, Toulon, Marseilles, Genoa and Spezzia, lost a few gold-pieces at Monte Carlo, and grew enthusiastic about *Faust*, the fashionable opera of the day. In April the Tsarevich George died at Nice, and Lesovsky's squadron had the duty of taking the body back to Russia. Rimsky-Korsakov, now a midshipman, returned to Kronstadt early in the summer of 1865. 'I had become an officer-dilettante, who sometimes enjoyed playing or listening to music; but all my dreams of artistic activity had completely flown away. Nor did I regret them'. He caught a few fleeting glimpses of Balakirev and his own family. But they spent the summer in the country, he at Kronstadt while the *Almaz* was being dismantled. In September he was transferred to St. Petersburg, where he took a furnished room.

Visiting Balakirev, however, Rimsky-Korsakov —ever susceptible to environment—began to renew his serious interest in music. He found all sorts of changes in the musical life of Petersburg. Balakirev's Free School, founded a few months before he had sailed, was now well established; the critic Serov had made a dramatic appearance as a composer with his *Judith*; the Balakirev circle had gained a new recruit in the chemistry professor of the Medical Academy, A. P. Borodin, who was already writing a symphony. As for Korsakov's own Symphony, Balakirev insisted on his finishing it by writing a trio to the scherzo (which he did in October) and reorchestrating the whole under his supervision. His naval duties consisted only of two or three hours' secretarial work each morning, so that he was able to devote plenty of time to music, spending much of his leisure at Balakirev's and sometimes even sleeping there. In November [1] he wrote his first published song, a setting of Heine's 'Lehn deine Wang' an meine Wang''. Balakirev approved of the melody but not of the accompaniment, and provided the song with an accompaniment of his own—with which it was printed.

[1] Not in December of the following year as he says in his memoirs. But the chronology of the memoirs is frequently incorrect, even the sequence of events being transposed.

CHAPTER III

1865–71

THE E flat minor Symphony—Rimsky-Korsakov's Op. 1—being finished, Balakirev decided to play it at one of his Free School concerts; and, after the two rehearsals then customary in Russia, the Symphony was given its first performance (in the distinguished company of Mozart's *Requiem*) on December 19th/31st, 1865. It was well received, and the audience were more than a little surprised when a young man in naval uniform appeared to take the applause. A second performance followed a month later at a Theatre Concert under Constantine Lyadov. At about the same time (January or February, 1866) Balakirev introduced his young friend to Glinka's sister, Lyudmila Shestakova, and from that time onward he was a frequent guest at her house. In her circle Rimsky-Korsakov made a number of fresh acquaintances, among others Dargomïzhsky and a singer, S. I. Zotova, whose performance inspired him to further essays in song-composition. In February, March and April, respectively, he wrote for her the well-known 'Nightingale enslaved by the rose', and settings of the cradle-song from

31

Mey's play *The Maid of Psov* and Heine's 'Aus
meinen Tränen', this time with his own accompaniments. With the earlier Heine song they
were published by Bernard in the summer as
Op. 2, though the composer did not receive a
kopek for them, and had to content himself with
the satisfaction of appearing in print for the first
time.

The summer brought forth not only a crop of
eight more songs (Opp. 3 and 4) but a new
orchestral piece, an *Overture on Three Russian
Themes*. (It is numbered Op. 28, but Rimsky-
Korsakov's opus-numbers are a quite unreliable
guide to the chronological order of his compositions.) Balakirev's preoccupation with the
harmonization of his collection of folk-songs that
spring had laid the foundation of Rimsky-
Korsakov's serious interest in folk-music, while
the melodies Balakirev had brought back from
the Caucasus attracted him to Oriental music.
The immediate fruit of his new interest was the
Overture, written during June and July. It was
modelled on Balakirev's two folk-song overtures
(the one in B minor and *Russia*) and two of the
themes were borrowed from his new collection of
Forty Folk-Songs, while the third is the well-known
one used by Beethoven in the second 'Razumovsky'
Quartet and Mussorgsky in the coronation scene
of *Boris*. The Overture was performed at a Free
School concert on December 11th/23rd, 1866,
together with Liszt's *Mephisto Waltz*, a work
which particularly fascinated Rimsky-Korsakov.

At the same time Korsakov was struggling
rather belatedly to improve his piano technique,

practising scales in thirds and octaves, working
industriously at Czerny's *Daily Exercises* and even
struggling with Chopin's studies. But Balakirev's
poor opinion of his pianistic ability frightened him
from playing before his musical friends, though
among his service comrades and in the family circle
at Voin's he was considered a 'beautiful pianist'.
At his brother's, too, he played for dancing on
Sunday evenings—quadrilles of his own composition on themes from *Martha* and *La belle Hélène*—
dark secrets which he kept from Balakirev. But
he seems to have found the company of the young
people who gathered at Voin's—his sister-in-law's
relations—more congenial than Lyudmila Shestakova's card-parties, where Balakirev was in his
element.

Both Cui and Balakirev agreed that Rimsky-
Korsakov showed a decided talent for orchestration, and 1867 saw not only the beginning of a
Second Symphony in B minor (which came to
nothing, though the scherzo in 5/4 time was used
in a later work) but the completion of two more
orchestral pieces, a *Fantasia on Serbian Themes*
written in a great hurry for Balakirev's Pan-
Slavonic Concert on May 12th/24th [1]—Balakirev's
Pan-Slavonic enthusiasm then being at its height,
just after his expedition to Prague—and the
'musical picture' *Sadko*, largely inspired by the
Liszt *Mephisto Waltz*. Rimsky-Korsakov began

[1] It was in his notice of this concert that Stassov inadvertently
gave the Balakirev group the nickname that stuck to it: 'God grant
that our Slavonic guests may never forget to-day's concert; God
grant that they may for ever preserve the memory of how much
poetry, feeling, talent and intelligence are possessed by the small
but already mighty handful' (*moguchaya kuchka*: literally, 'mighty
little-heap') 'of Russian musicians'.

C

Sadko in June during a three-weeks' holiday at his brother's summer villa at Tervayoki, near Vyborg, was obliged to interrupt it for a month's cruise in the Gulf of Finland, and finished it on September 30th/October 12th. Announcing this piece of news to Mussorgsky, the next youngest member of the circle, with whom he had lately been drawn into more intimate personal friendship, he says: 'I don't mind telling you that I'm perfectly satisfied with it; it's decidedly the best thing I've done, considerably better even than that *andante* of the Symphony which took me such a devil of a time to write. . . . So *Sadko* is finished and I owe you my best thanks, Modest, for the idea—which you gave me, I remember, at Cui's the night before his wife went to Minsk.[1] Once more: thank you. Now I'm going to rest, for my noddle's a bit weary from the intense strain; I'm going to rest, be idle, write a few songs, and after that—I don't know myself, but I doubt if the B minor *allegro*' (of the projected Second Symphony) 'will be resuscitated from the ashes—still, one never knows! Mily is quite satisfied with *Sadko* and didn't want to make any comments'. All these orchestral works were written for the old-fashioned 'natural' horns and trumpets as described in Berlioz's *Traité*, the composer writing for horns in every possible crook and getting tied in all sorts of knots in trying to avoid 'stopped' notes. As Korsakov said afterwards: 'It would have been altogether beneath our dignity to have consulted some practical musician who would have put us right.

[1] The idea of a musical treatment of the Sadko legend was originally suggested by Stassov to Balakirev in 1861.

We were the brothers-in-arms of Berlioz, not of some ungifted bandmaster. . . .'

That winter Berlioz, himself, came to Russia again, on Balakirev's invitation, to conduct six concerts for the Russian Music Society. But Rimsky-Korsakov had no chance of meeting the man whose chief rival in orchestral virtuosity he was destined to become. Berlioz was a sick man throughout the visit, spending most of his free time lying down—'ill with 18 horse-power, coughing like six donkeys with the glanders', as he wrote to the Massarts—and had no relations with any Russian musicians except Balakirev, Cui, the Stassovs and the Directors of the Russian Music Society. He died a year later. But Balakirev himself was the Society's conductor-in-chief that season; he gave the first performance of *Sadko* on December 9th/21st, 1867, and also played the *Serbian Fantasia* again—both works winning the unstinted praise of the usually hostile Serov.

Rimsky-Korsakov was still living in a furnished room on Vassily Island, going to his brother's for meals and spending his evenings at Balakirev's, Borodin's or Lodïzhensky's, or with Mussorgsky. Less often with Cui. And that spring, the spring of 1868, the whole circle found a new weekly rendezvous at Dargomïzhsky's, where they heard and performed his remarkable essay in operatic realism, *The Stone Guest*. In this house the twenty-four-year-old Rimsky-Korsakov made the acquaintance of the sisters Alexandra and Nadezhda Purgold, aged respectively twenty-four and twenty. Alexandra was a singer, an excellent amateur, Nadezhda a pianist, who had studied

under Mussorgsky's old teacher Herke and at the
St. Petersburg Conservatoire under Zaremba.
Before very long the members of the Balakirev
circle were visiting the Purgolds. (The family
consisted of the sisters, their mother and uncle;
while there were other married sisters and
brothers.) These visits led to the most important
consequences for Rimsky-Korsakov. But he seems
never to have been much of a ladies' man; the
great romance of his life, a most domestic, not to
say bourgeois, affair, was apparently not the result
of love at first sight.

His head was full of plans. Within three
months of the completion of *Sadko* he was thinking
of a 'symphony or four-movement symphonic
poem' based on Senkovsky's Oriental tale *Antar*,
and the first and fourth movements were written
during January and February, 1868. He already
had an idea for an opera on that play of Mey's,
The Maid of Pskov, from which he had taken the
text of one of his first songs. But for the moment
he concentrated on *Antar*, his 'Second Symphony'
as he called it originally. (In 1903, when he
brought out a new edition, it was restyled
'symphonic suite'.) As he said afterwards, 'the
term "suite" was at that time practically unknown to our circle. . . . Still I had no right to
call *Antar* a symphony. My *Antar* was a poem,
suite, legend, anything you like, but not a
symphony'. It was during the composition of
Antar, he tells us, that he first ventured to offer
mild resistance to Balakirev's despotic interference in his work. He was at last beginning to
feel able to stand on his own feet and assert his

own artistic will. Another and more curious sign of ripening musical individuality was that sense of the colour associations of musical keys which began to awaken in him at this period and which afterwards exercised over him an influence amounting almost to tyranny.

The second movement of *Antar* was written in June. Most of Rimsky-Korsakov's friends and relations having left Petersburg for the country, he was left rather sadly with the not too congenial company of Dargomïzhsky and Cui—who took the opportunity to get him to orchestrate the opening chorus of his opera, *William Ratcliffe*. As usual, during the summer months Nicholas occupied Voin's deserted quarters in the Naval College. One day he made an expedition with Dargomïzhsky and the Cuis to the Purgolds' summer villa and, being rather bored and lonely, drifted back again and again—alone. (Of two songs written that summer, one was tactfully dedicated to Nadezhda, the other to Alexandra.) Then one day, early in July, came an invitation to join the Borodins, who were staying on Lodïzhensky's estate in the Tver Government. 'I remember how, sitting alone in my brother's flat, I - received Lodïzhensky's invitation. I remember how the prospect of a journey into the solitudes of the very heart of Russia instantaneously evoked in me an overwhelming sensation of love for the life of the Russian people, for their history in general, and for *The Maid of Pskov* in particular; and how, under the impression of that emotion, I went to the piano and immediately improvised the theme of the chorus with which the people greet Tsar Ivan'. After three weeks in the country, riding and walking with his hosts and the Borodins—and 'eating an awful lot of berries and cream', as he wrote to Mussorgsky—and another week at Tervayoki with his family, he returned to Petersburg in August, and wrote the third movement of *Antar* and several numbers of the First Act of *The Maid of Pskov*. Both *Antar* and the 'Greeting Chorus' from *The Maid* were given that winter at Russian Music Society concerts, under Balakirev. (It was the last season he conducted for the Society.) Rimsky-Korsakov himself had been invited to conduct his compositions and had applied to his commanding officer for permission to do so. But Krabbe, the Minister of Marine, solemnly declared that 'It is not agreeable to His Imperial Majesty that his officers should appear publicly as performers at concerts, any more than in theatrical representations'. So Rimsky-Korsakov had to content himself with appearing on the platform to take the applause.

The production of Cui's *William Ratcliffe* in February, 1869, was the occasion of Rimsky-Korsakov's only two excursions into the field of musical journalism. Cui, being busy with rehearsals, induced Borodin and Rimsky-Korsakov to devil for him as critic of the *St. Petersburg Vedomosti*, and it fell to the latter's lot to criticize not only *Ratcliffe* itself, but a new opera by Napravnik, who had just succeeded Constantine Lyadov as chief conductor at the Maryinsky Theatre. Full of the prevalent ideas of operatic realism, Rimsky-Korsakov ridiculed the con-

ventionalism of Napravnik's work and amused
himself (if not his readers) by pointing out the
unfortunate wealth of reminiscence in the music.
To the end of his life he blamed this youthful
indiscretion for spoiling his relations with a fine
artist, who for many years was to be one of the
outstanding figures in Russian musical life,
particularly in the sphere of opera. (Indeed,
almost immediately after this, Napravnik succeeded Balakirev as conductor of the Russian
Music Society.)

Dargomïzhsky having died in January, 1869,
Rimsky-Korsakov began, in accordance with the
composer's wish, the scoring of *The Stone Guest*.
His own *Maid* progressed—rather slowly. And
he revised the orchestration of *Sadko*, the first
sign of that profound self-dissatisfaction, revealed
in the constant working over of old material,
which flowed in such a strong undercurrent
throughout the remainder of his career. Given
in this new version at a Free School concert, *Sadko*
was even more successful than before. 'The
public was enraptured', Borodin wrote to his wife.
'Korsinka was called out three times'. Even
Serov wrote that 'Mr. Rimsky-Korsakov, alone of
all his party, gifted with enormous talent . . .
glitters amid his unfortunate entourage like a
diamond among cobble-stones'. But trouble with
his eyes condemned Rimsky-Korsakov to a long
stretch of inactivity at this period. An expedition
to Moscow with Balakirev in January, 1870, and
a two months' holiday at Tervayoki with his
mother in the following summer—the Purgold
girls being on holiday in the West—were the only

breaks in an uneventful routine of service duties.
The orchestration of *The Stone Guest* was finished at
Tervayoki; some more songs appeared—those
published as Op. 8; and by February, 1871, *The
Maid of Pskov* was sketched out and the orchestra-
tion begun. Then, after three months of un-
explained idleness, the scoring was resumed in
June and the first two acts, with the first scene of
Act III, completed by September.

Contrary to his usual custom, Mussorgsky spent
the summer of 1871 in St. Petersburg, and,
delighted to have his company, Rimsky-Korsakov
frequently took him to Voin's. And they often
went together to visit Stassov and the Purgold
girls, motherless since the previous December, who
had summer villas at Pargolovo. This was the
period of their closest friendship. And fate was
to bring them even closer for a while. Voin
Rimsky-Korsakov's health, long bad, took a turn
for the worse that autumn and his doctor ordered
him abroad. Shutting up his flat, he set out with
his wife and children for Italy; his mother went
to Moscow to live; and Nicholas decided to join
forces with Mussorgsky. The two youngest
members of the 'mighty handful' lived together
that winter in a single room, Mussorgsky revising
and adding to *Boris*, Rimsky-Korsakov scoring the
Fourth Act and Overture of *The Maid of Pskov*.
Yet already in the summer of 1871 Rimsky-
Korsakov had taken a step which was the direct
cause of Mussorgsky's gradual estrangement from
him a year or so later, a step which was to lead
to a complete change of direction in his musical
development.

CHAPTER IV

1871–76

Offered professorship in St Petersburg – technical ignorance – acceptance after doubts – successful bluff – death of Voin Rimsky-Korsakov – betrothal to Nadezhda Purgold – her influence – the collective *Mlada* – *The Maid of Pskov* causes trouble with the censorship – marriage – production of *The Maid of Pskov* – Rimsky-Korsakov leaves the Navy – becomes civilian Inspector of Naval Bands – studies wind-instruments – self-education in harmony and counterpoint – Third Symphony – birth of first child – début as conductor – becomes Director of Free School of Music – in the Crimea – preoccupation with academic counterpoint – second version of *Antar* – defects as a conductor.

'ONE fine day', Rimsky-Korsakov tells us in his autobiography, 'I received a visit from Azanchevsky, newly appointed to the Directorship of the St. Petersburg Conservatoire in succession to Zaremba. To my surprise he invited me to accept the Professorship of Practical Composition and Instrumentation and the direction of the orchestral class, with a salary of one thousand rubles' (roughly, £100 a year). During the four years, 1867–71, that Rubinstein's successor Zaremba had reigned over the Conservatoire, these branches of study had got into a bad state and Azanchevsky seems to have had the bright idea of enlivening them by introducing young blood in the person of this twenty-seven-year-old naval officer, who had attracted such favourable notice by his 'ultramodern' orchestral pieces. He knew Rimsky-Korsakov to be an amateur, but he cannot have had an inkling of the incredible truth. 'It was not merely that I couldn't at that time have harmonized a chorale properly, had never written a single contrapuntal exercise in my life, and had only the haziest understanding of strict fugue; but I didn't even know the names of the augmented and diminished intervals or of the chords, other than the tonic triad and the dominant and diminished sevenths; though I could sing anything at sight and *distinguish* every conceivable chord, the terms "chord of the sixth" and "six-four chords" were unknown to me. In my compositions I strove after correct part-writing and achieved it by instinct and by ear. My grasp of the musical forms (particularly of the rondo) was equally hazy. Although I scored my own compositions colourfully enough, I had no real knowledge of the technique of the strings, or of the practical possibilities of horns, trumpets and trombones. As for conducting, I had never conducted an orchestra in my life. . . .'

To do him justice, Rimsky-Korsakov did hesitate at first. But 'my friends advised me to accept. Even Balakirev, who alone really knew how unprepared I was, took the same view— being chiefly influenced by the wish to *get a footing* in the hostile Conservatoire'. Moreover, Korsakov himself was 'young and self-confident' and ignorant of his own ignorance. 'I agreed. In the autumn I was to become a professor at the Conservatoire without taking off my naval uniform'. In a letter to his mother (July 15th/ 27th) he reckons up the advantages the position will bring him: 'First, pecuniary; second, I shall be occupied with matters which give me pleasure and for which I am most adapted; third, it will be good practice for me, particularly as regards the conducting; and finally, here is a chance of definitely launching myself on a musical career and leaving the service, to continue in which for long I do not consider altogether fair and honest. Taking all this into consideration, I have agreed to go to the Conservatoire'. (It appears not to have occurred to him that it was not 'altogether fair and honest' to accept this new post.) And so the appointment was made. Nor was it the first instance of an utter incompetent being given such a post in Russia, for in 1834 Gogol had been appointed Professor of History in Petersburg University with no more knowledge of history than Rimsky-Korsakov had of musical theory. But whereas Gogol failed miserably, and was obliged to resign, Rimsky-Korsakov bluffed his way through with astounding success.

As he said, none of his pupils could have suspected his ignorance at first; he put them off with commonplaces, eked out by his personal tastes and his practical experience; and by the time they had begun to find him out, he had already learned something. Later he did teach himself to some purpose. 'And so, undeservedly given a professorship in the Conservatoire, I soon became one of its best pupils—perhaps the best of all—as regards the quantity and quality of the knowledge I acquired there'. And few will dispute the fact that this most incompetent of professors made himself a very great teacher, the greatest composition teacher (except perhaps Taneev) Russia has so far managed to produce.[1]

[1] Rimsky-Korsakov seems to have been adored by all his later pupils. Sokolov, who entered his class at the Conservatoire

But that was not yet. The Rimsky-Korsakov who shared a room with Mussorgsky and composed the original version of *The Maid of Pskov* was a young man whose self-confidence had far outrun his ability, and who was now rather frightened at the extent of his own ignorance and perhaps already secretly a little ashamed of the course of humbug in which his temerity had involved him.

That winter the pattern of Rimsky-Korsakov's life was shot through with other, most varied colours in generous compensation for the drab monotony of the last two or three years. First a streak of black. On November 4th/16th, 1871, Voin Rimsky-Korsakov died at Pisa; Nicholas had lost his second father. He was at once despatched to Italy by the Ministry of Marine to bring home the Admiral's embalmed body. (It is characteristic of Rimsky-Korsakov's cool, phlegmatic temperament that in the middle of this sad duty he found time to call on Anton Rubinstein in Vienna and hear him play through Liszt's *Christus*.) But Voin's death had one most unexpected consequence, for Nicholas suddenly found himself the favourite of Krabbe, the Minister of Marine. Krabbe, a good courtier and bad sailor, great lover of music and the theatre—and still greater lover of pretty actresses, had been Voin's determined and lifelong antagonist. But no sooner was Voin dead than he good-naturedly

in 1878, was 'at once charmed by his simple, utterly un-"professorial" manner, his childlike capacity for rejoicing over a good piece of work and being very deeply distressed by our failures. I am not ashamed to confess that Rimsky-Korsakov's outward appearance—his ill-cut, shabby clothes and his old boots—complied with the unconscious demands of my democratic leanings' (*Reminiscences of Rimsky-Korsakov*).

took the warmest interest in his family, saw that his mother, widow and children were well provided for, and, sending for Nicholas, assured him of his friendship and help in case of difficulty. Before long Nicholas was glad to avail himself of Krabbe's help, though in a matter quite unconnected with the service.

On the day after his arrival in Pisa, Rimsky-Korsakov had written to Nadezhda Purgold: 'Coming home from your house that last evening, I was so upset that I forgot myself and wrote to you almost in a state of fever, and now this letter presents itself to my mind in a sort of fog, but I will only say that I don't withdraw a single word of that letter. The next day I left Petersburg with an extremely painful feeling; though naturally fatigue and travel impressions blurred it. I thought about you a great deal on the way . . . and when I happened to see something nice, I always wanted you to look at it with me'. It needs no great skill to read between such lines as those, and one is not surprised to learn that they were betrothed the next month.

From this point—if not, of course, before—the influence of Nadezhda (a far better trained musician than himself, we must remember) began to play a very important part in Rimsky-Korsakov's musical development. He said little about it himself, but his friends recognized it. Next to Balakirev, who was just on the eve of the breakdown which for years removed him from Russian musical life, Nadezhda was the chief formative influence in his life. She was a quiet woman but one with very decided artistic views; she did not hesitate to. alter Tchaïkovsky's *Romeo and Juliet* when transcribing it for piano. Nor were her own musical activities limited to piano-playing and the wholesale transcription of contemporary Russian orchestral works. She was a composer herself until the growth of her family obliged her to lay musical work aside. Only a week or two before her marriage she completed a 'musical picture', *The Enchanted Spot*, based on one of Gogol's *Evenings on a Farm near Dikanka*, which she orchestrated the following year. And her enthusiasm for Gogol's *Evenings* is reflected in the subjects of her husband's works and those of his friends. On the day of their betrothal Nadezhda and Nicholas read *May Night* together and she was very anxious that he should write an opera on it. And a week or two later she wrote to him: 'I've been reading yet another of Gogol's stories to-day, *The Fair of Sorochintsy*. This is good, too, and would even be suitable for an opera, but not for *you*; in any case, it's not like *May Night*. As for *that*, it's so stuck in my head that nothing will drive it out'. She, or her sister, at once suggested *The Fair* to Mussorgsky, who turned it down at the time but returned to it a couple of years later.

In the meantime Rimsky-Korsakov was busy with other operatic matters. In February, 1872, *The Stone Guest* was produced and he eagerly attended the rehearsals to study the effect of his orchestration. Then, perhaps in consequence of his contact with the young nationalist composers in the course of *The Stone Guest* rehearsals, S. A. Gedeonov, the director of the Imperial Theatres, commissioned from them—that is, from Cui,

Borodin, Mussorgsky and Rimsky-Korsakov—an
'opera-ballet' *Mlada,* for which he himself supplied
a scenario, to be composed collectively. Acts II
and III were divided between Mussorgsky and
Rimsky-Korsakov, who were still sharing a room,
but the project soon fell through, and in any case
Rimsky-Korsakov must have been much more
concerned with the fate of *The Maid of Pskov*
'completed in January) which was still undecided.
The libretto had been sent to the dramatic censor,
who was making all sorts of difficulties. For
one thing, the picture of the semi-independent,
republican constitution of the city of Pskov in the
year 1570 was considered highly objectionable.
Instead of a free city defending its rights, Pskov
had to be shown as a rebellious city. Again,
Ivan the Terrible was one of the principal characters, and according to an edict of Nicholas I,
in 1837, pre-Romanov Russian rulers might be
represented on the stage in drama or tragedy *but
not in opera,* since it would never do for a tsar to be
shown doing anything so undignified as singing.
From this impasse Rimsky-Korsakov escaped by a
typically Russian avenue. He turned to his new
friend, the Minister of Marine. Krabbe was as
good as his word; the machinery of Court
favouritism began to work, and the interest of the
Grand Duke Constantine Nikolaevich, the Tsar's
brother, was enlisted on behalf of the new opera.
It is true Rimsky-Korsakov had to give way in the
matter of the republican popular assembly, but
all other difficulties vanished. The Directorate
of the Imperial Theatres accepted the work at
once, in spite of the fact (according to Solovyev

and other unfriendly newspaper critics) that, like
Boris, it had been rejected by the selection committee. In the meantime, *The Maid*, like most
of the other new Russian operas of the period,
was tried out privately in the composer's own
circle, both at Krabbe's and at the Purgolds',
Mussorgsky, Korsakov and the sisters all taking
part.

Early in the summer of 1872 Rimsky-Korsakov
left the apartment he had been sharing with
Mussorgsky and took a room at Pargolovo, so as
to be near his fiancée. On June 30th/July 12th
they were married, Mussorgsky acting as best
man, and went abroad for their honeymoon.
They spent July in Switzerland and among the
Italian lakes, then in Milan and Venice, returning to Russia by way of Vienna and Warsaw in
the middle of August. After a round of visits to
relations they settled down in their house in
Petersburg early in the autumn. Nicholas was
twenty-eight, Nadezhda four years younger.

Owing to their absence abroad the proof-
reading of the vocal score of *The Maid*, made by
Nadezhda, had been left to Cui, who had done it
very carelessly. Consequently the very rare first
edition (published by Bessel) has a fine crop of
misprints in both words and music, misprints
which were the joy of unfriendly critics. N. F.
Solovyev, for instance, pouncing on an incorrectly
printed tremolo, acidly remarked that 'such
ignorance of an elementary rule is rather surprising in the publication of a production by a
professor of the Conservatoire'. Rehearsals began
in the autumn, not too happily. Napravnik,

thorough and conscientious as ever, was not quite successful in concealing his dislike of the work, which, like *Boris*, was a compromise between melodic, folk-songish opera of the Glinka type and realistic 'truth' in the manner of *The Stone Guest*. (Moreover, the original *Maid of Pskov* was a very much cruder affair than the version which, as *Ivan the Terrible*, has reached Western Europe.) Petrov, who sang Ivan, was also dissatisfied with his part. But the first performance on January 1st/13th, 1873, at the Maryinsky Theatre (for the benefit of Platonova, who sang the heroine) was entirely successful. The composer was called out 'ten or fifteen times', according to Solovyev, and in spite of a bad press the opera was given nine times more before the season came to an end six weeks later. The revolutionary element in it, as in *Boris*, captured the young people and Borodin's students sang the rebel chorus from the Second Act about the corridors of the Army Medical Academy.

That might easily have had unpleasant consequences for the composer. But at this period Rimsky-Korsakov could hardly do anything wrong in the eyes of the authorities. Krabbe even created a new post with a handsome salary specially for him, that of Inspector of Naval Bands, and so put an end to the anomaly of a serving naval lieutenant who was also a professor at a musical conservatoire. Accordingly, in May, Rimsky-Korsakov took off his uniform and became a civil official with the rank of 'collegiate assessor'. He was delighted with his new duties and entered upon them with a certain excess of

D

zeal, bewildering the good bandmasters with his ridicule of the pearls of their repertoire, and hunting down bad instruments and wrong notes in the band-parts ('of which there were a great many', he remarks) with the exuberance of a witch-doctor smelling out evil spirits. 'The bands treated me as "authority"—standing to attention', he recollected with naïve pleasure. In short, he made himself the terror of every naval band in Petersburg and Kronstadt. The fact that he knew very little about the technique of the band instruments was not the sort of thing to discourage a man like Rimsky-Korsakov, but it is characteristic that he at once set to work to study the instruments for himself. When he and Nadezhda went to Pargolovo for the summer, he took with him a trombone, flute, clarinet and one or two other instruments, with a collection of diagrams and tutors, and 'regardless of the neighbours', as he said, learned, if not to play them, at least *how* they were played. It is equally characteristic that, with this very elementary knowledge, he at once began to plan a colossal treatise on instrumentation, a book that was to contain a lengthy monograph on each instrument with innumerable sketches and tables and diagrams explaining the mechanism which he hardly understood himself. From Tyndall and Helmholtz he cooked up an introduction dealing with the acoustic laws underlying the construction of the instruments, and worked at this *magnum opus* off and on for two years before he finally abandoned it. Yet this was not wasted labour. He learned from it and from his inter-

course with the naval bands 'what' (as he said)
'every German military bandmaster knows but
what, unfortunately, artist-composers don't know':
'the difference between virtuoso-difficulties and
impracticabilities' on each instrument. His natural
sense of orchestral colour was gradually being
reinforced by practical knowledge—a formidable
combination, as he was to prove later.

Then, again, he was teaching himself harmony
and counterpoint, studying the former from
Tchaïkovsky's text-book, the latter from Cheru-
bini's *Cours* and G. H. Bellermann's treatise. The
Conservatoire Professor of Composition, composer
of a successful opera and several successful
orchestral works, conscientiously worked innumerable figured basses and *canti fermi* and
harmonized countless simple melodies like any
beginner, gradually educating himself during
the next year or two, till by 1875 he could
write a fugue as well as any fairly advanced
counterpoint student at a German conservatoire.
But in the meantime he was unable to resist
the temptation to embody his dangerous 'little
learning' in practical composition. Just as he
had embarked on his great treatise when he had
only just begun to understand the mechanism
of the instruments, he now—with only the most
elementary knowledge of counterpoint—began
nothing less than a symphony full of contrapuntal
tricks, theme-combinations and so on. For the
scherzo he used the old scherzo in 5/4 time,
composed for the projected B minor Symphony
of 1867 (and now provided with a trio composed
during a steamer trip on one of the Italian lakes

during his honeymoon). He worked at this
so-called 'Third' Symphony in C major during
that summer of 1873 at Pargolovo in the intervals
of his tours of band-inspection and his very
immature flutings and trombonings. In August
the imminence of what is popularly considered
a happy event sent the Rimsky-Korsakovs back
to Petersburg, no doubt to the great joy of everyone within earshot, and on the 20th (September
1st) Nadezhda presented her husband with their
first child, Michael ('Misha').[1]

Rimsky-Korsakov had for some time been
conducting the orchestral class at the Conservatoire, but so far he had never made a public
appearance as a conductor. However, he was
asked that winter to conduct a choral and
orchestral concert in aid of the Samara famine
sufferers. He agreed and, after worrying himself
nearly to death for a month beforehand, made
a fairly successful début (February 18th/March
2nd, 1874), satisfying almost everyone but the
soloists he had to accompany. His programme
was an all-Russian one with two novelties, his
own new Symphony and the new version of
Mussorgsky's *Destruction of Sennacherib*. Cui hailed
the Symphony as 'the best of all Mr. Korsakov's
productions—the fruit of ripe thought, happy
inspiration and strong talent combined with deep
and solid technical knowledge'. But the rest of

[1] 'Misha' became a Professor of Zoology. There were six
other children: Sonya (b. 1875), Andrey (b. 1878), the famous
musicologist, head of the Leningrad Public Library, Vladimir
('Volodya') (b. 1882), Nadya (b. 1884), who married the
composer Steinberg, Masha (b. 1888), who died at the age of
five, and Slavchik (b. 1889), who died when only twelve months
old.

his friends disagreed. They simply thought it dull—and posterity has agreed with them. Even Borodin, more sympathetic than most, said it was very evidently the work of a professor who had put on his spectacles to write '*Eine grosse Symphonie in C*'.

Just before this concert Rimsky-Korsakov received from Balakirev, in his retirement, a very warm and affectionate letter wishing him success. But Balakirev, though he had completely disappeared from the musical world, had not resigned the Directorship of the Free School of Music, and that unfortunate institution, deprived of its founder and chief, was nearly bankrupt and slowly dying. Possibly as a consequence of Rimsky-Korsakov's appearance as a conductor, some of the members of the committee saw an opportunity of saving the wreck, induced Balakirev to resign, and offered the Directorship to Rimsky-Korsakov, who accepted it in May, though he was unable to devote much time to the work till the following autumn and winter.

It was at this period that Mussorgsky began to regard Rimsky-Korsakov as a 'traitor' to his old ideals. Their intimacy was beginning to be spoiled and Korsakov drew correspondingly nearer to Borodin, enlisting him as a fellow-student of instrumental technique. He seldom appeared at Borodin's for the evening without some wind instrument which they 'studied together and amused themselves with'. Rimsky-Korsakov also set about enriching the repertoire of the brass and wood-wind naval bands and transcribed a number of works by Glinka, Meyerbeer, and others—the

Lohengrin Prelude among the rest.   In the summer
he went with his wife and baby to Nikolaev on the
Black Sea to reorganize the band of the naval
garrison there.   (Russia had recently denounced
the Treaty of Paris which forbade her to maintain
a Black Sea Fleet.)   From Nikolaev they crossed
by steamer to Sevastopol and visited the south of
the Crimea.   In Bakhchisaray, where there was
then no hotel and they had to stay with some
mullah opposite the famous Fountain of Tears
which inspired Pushkin's *Fountain of Bakhchisaray*,
Rimsky-Korsakov heard genuine Eastern music
for the first time.   He was deeply impressed by it
and by what he calls the 'gypsy-musicians' who
played in the streets from morning to night.
When he returned to Bakhchisaray seven years
later he was disgusted to find that the un-
imaginative authorities had suppressed these
picturesque minstrels as public nuisances.

Returning to St. Petersburg Rimsky-Korsakov
organized and conducted in October a concert
by the massed naval bands of the Petersburg and
Kronstadt commands and took in hand the
revitalization of the Free School.   He got a choir
together and in March, 1875, gave a concert: the
first Free School concert since Balakirev's dis-
appearance in 1872.   But the programme was
very different from the old 'ultra-modern' Free
School programmes.   Rimsky-Korsakov, in the
course of his contrapuntal studies, had discovered
Bach and Palestrina, and the one-time progressivist
staggered Petersburg with a programme in which
the most modern composer was Haydn.   The rest
was all Palestrina and Allegri, excerpts from *Israel*

in Egypt and three arias and the final chorus from Bach's *Matthew Passion* (two of them heard for the first time in Russia.) Korsakov pursued his own contrapuntal studies with exceptional industry that spring and summer, working his exercises even on the Petersburg-Kronstadt steamer as he went on his visits of inspection. That summer the exercises flowered—if that is the right word—into six fugues for piano, published as Op. 17, which he humbly submitted to his colleague, the theorist, Johannsen, for approval, and two three-part female choruses, Op. 13. They had already produced more monstrous fruit in a String Quartet in F, Op. 12, a first essay in chamber music which was performed by the Auer Quartet the following November. Anton Rubinstein thought it 'showed promise' and Tchaïkovsky expressed inordinate admiration for the first movement, but the composer himself knew better. He was frankly ashamed of his 'incessant fugato'—'I felt involuntarily that in this Quartet I was really not myself. . . . Technique had not yet entered into my flesh and blood'—and he stayed away from the concert.

1875 was indeed a critical year for Rimsky-Korsakov. Others besides Mussorgsky considered him a 'traitor' to the cause of progress. In fact all his old friends except Borodin regarded him as a lost soul. Balakirev was moved by the Free School concert programme to write him bitter reproaches for his 'spiritual flabbiness', while Stassov wrote to Golenishchev-Kutuzov (September, 1875): 'The Roman [1] has not been sitting

---

[1] *Rimlyanin*: a play on Rimsky-Korsakov's name. *Rimsky* is the Russian adjective 'Roman'.

with folded hands; he has written sixty-one
fugues (!!!) and a dozen or so canons.[1] I won't
comment. *De mortuis. . . .*' Only Borodin, who
had himself just horrified Stassov and Mussorgsky
by beginning a string quartet—chamber music
being frowned on in those quarters—took a
different view. 'Korsinka is fussing about with
the Free School', he wrote to Lyubov Karmalina
(April 15th/27th, 1875), 'writing all sorts of
counterpoints, learning and teaching all sorts of
musical tricks. He's writing a course of instrumentation—phenomenal, there's never been anything like it; but he has no time at present and
has laid it aside till he has some leisure. . . . For
the present he is not writing any music. . . . A
lot of people are up in arms because Korsakov has
turned back and taken to the study of musical
antiquity. But that doesn't worry me. It's quite
understandable: Korsakov developed in just the
opposite way from me. He began with Glinka,
Liszt and Berlioz—well, being surfeited with them,
it's only natural that he should turn to a field
which is unknown to him and still has the interest
of novelty'. As for Tchaïkovsky, he considered
'these innumerable contrapuntal exercises, these
sixty fugues [2] and the host of other musical tricks
—such a feat for the man who had written *Sadko*
eight years before', such 'heroic exploits', that he
wanted 'to proclaim it to the whole world', to
'bow down before' the other's 'artistic modesty

---

[1] According to Borodin, in a letter of only a week earlier, it was
'36 fugues and 16 canons'.

[2] How the number varies! Rimsky-Korsakov himself said
later that the rumour that he had written *fifty* fugues was 'a little
exaggerated', though he had forgotten the exact number.

and strength of character'. (Though it is true Tchaïkovsky anticipated correctly, if he did not already know, that Rimsky-Korsakov would be one of the judges in the opera competition for which he had just submitted his *Vakula the Smith*.) But there was a real danger that in 'making technique part of his flesh and blood', Korsakov would entirely kill his own spontaneous creative talent. With his wife seriously ill from the birth of their second child, Sonya, he buried himself in his exercise-books and went on manufacturing dry little piano pieces (Op. 15) and *a capella* choruses (Op. 16). He even tortured a Russian folk-song into *Four Variations and a Fughetta* for four-part female choir, inflicting all these ingenuities on the Free School choral class.

He blushed for the 'harmonic impurities' of his *Antar*, cleaned them up, entirely reorchestrated the work and, in this new form, conducted it at an R.M.S. concert in January, 1876. This was the first time the Society had played one of his compositions since Balakirev's departure, and even now Napravnik had declined to conduct *Antar* himself. Of the Free School concerts that season, the first (in February) was nearly all Bach and Handel,[1] while the second was entirely devoted to Russian music—which rehabilitated him in the eyes of his friends but wiped out the financial profit on the first concert. At the rehearsals, as he faithfully confesses in his memoirs, he occasion-

---

[1] The 'Kyrie', 'Qui sedes', 'Crucifixus' and 'Dona nobis' from the B minor Mass; and 'Then round about the starry throne', 'My faith and truth', 'Hear, Jacob's God', 'Great Dagon', 'Weep, Israel, weep', 'Glorious hero' and 'Let their celestial concerts' from *Samson*.

ally lost his temper and spoke in a 'too commanding tone', a slip which he attributes to his naval
habits.   But the truth is that he was exceptionally
mild and easy-going as a conductor and, on his
own showing, a far from reliable one: losing his
place in Beethoven's Fifth Symphony, bungling
starts, and performing other feats of the same
nature.

CHAPTER V

1876–87

Collections of folk-songs – begins *Record of my Musical Life* — collaborates in editing Glinka's operas – second version of *The Maid of Pskov* – *May Night* – the *Paraphrases* – Free School concerts – *Snow Maiden* – 'praying to nature' → pantheism – *Legend* for orchestra and *Sinfonietta on Russian Themes* – Mussorgsky's death – Rimsky-Korsakov supervises publication of his works – in the Crimea again – resigns Directorship of Free School of Music – work on Mussorgsky's *Khovanshchina* – meeting with Belaev – Piano Concerto – Assistant Music Director of the Imperial Chapel – period of sterility – the Belaev circle – Belaev turns publisher and founds the Russian Symphony Concerts – First and Third Symphonies revised and reorchestrated – writes harmony text-book – *B-la-F* Quartet and *Fantasia on Russian Themes*.

RIMSKY - KORSAKOV'S rescue from bone - dry academicism was effected by two main agencies, his study of folk-song and the editing of Glinka's opera scores. Already in 1875 he had been thinking of making a collection of folk-songs; now through Balakirev, who was beginning to reappear rather furtively in musical circles, he was approached by the latter's friend, T. I. Filippov, to collaborate in such a collection. Filippov was a keen amateur of folk-songs and Korsakov noted down forty of them from his singing and provided them with piano-accompaniments, work which had to be done all over again since the first version was 'not simple and Russian enough' to satisfy him.[1] But the songs Filippov knew were mostly lyrical and comparatively modern, while Rimsky-Korsakov was much more

[1] For some reason the collection was not published till 1882.

interested in the ritual songs and singing games originally connected with ancient pagan customs, principally with the old Slavonic sun-worship. So, having dealt with Filippov's collection, he pressed ahead with his own monumental *Collection of One Hundred Russian Folk-Songs*, most of the work being done in 1876, though not actually completed till November, 1877. He took and reharmonized a number of the songs from older collections like that of Ivan Prach, while the rest came from his mother, friends and acquaintances, and his recollections of his Uncle Peter. One of the most valuable collaborators—and almost the only genuine peasant contributor—was the Borodins' maid, Dunyasha, the 'A. E. Vinogradova' whose help is acknowledged. On one occasion Korsakov sat late into the night trying to get the right rhythmic notation for one of her songs (No. 72). The harmonization also gave him a great deal of trouble. Melgunov did not startle Russian musicians with his revolutionary, but perfectly correct, theory of the polyphonic nature of Russian folk-music till three or four years later, and Rimsky-Korsakov had no idea that his own 'truly Russian' harmonizations were on the wrong track. (In any case, when Melgunov's collection did appear, Rimsky-Korsakov thought it 'barbarous'.) But it has long been recognized that his famous collection, valuable as it is artistically, is far from authentic as a scientific record of Russian folk-music. Nevertheless his study of the old customs in which so many of the songs had originated was to have an extraordinarily fertilising effect on his own creative imagination. 'Pictures of the old

pagan days and their spirit arose before my mind's
eye with great clearness, and attracted me
irresistibly'.

But for the time being he remained entangled
in terribly contrapuntal chamber music, the
String Sextet in A and the Quintet in B flat for
piano and wind. Both were submitted for a
competition promoted by the R.M.S.—and both
were unsuccessful. That summer, too, he wrote
the first chapter of his fascinating, if not in every
respect completely reliable, *Record of my Musical
Life*, though, having made this beginning, he laid
the manuscript aside for eleven or twelve years.
He also wrote two mixed choruses (Op. 18) and
some unaccompanied male choruses (Op. 23)
that summer, and planned a sort of Handelian
cantata, *Alexander Nevsky*, to words by Mey. A
little later came some even more wonderful
compositions: a Trombone Concerto, *Variations
on a Theme of Glinka's* for oboe, and a *Concertstück* for clarinet, all with wind - band accompaniment—written, of course, for the naval
bands.

It was at this period, the autumn of 1876, that
Balakirev once more began to play an active part
in Rimsky-Korsakov's life. Balakirev sent him
private pupils in elementary theory, mostly
dabbling young ladies who benefited Korsakov's
pocket more than their own musical culture,[1]
and invited him and his young pupil, Anatol
Lyadov, to collaborate with him in the magnificent
edition of Glinka's operas which he was preparing

[1] Among them a certain Mme. Glazunova, who in December,
1879, also sent along her fourteen-year-old son, Alexander.

on the commission of Lyudmila Shestakova. The work occupied them, off and on, for four years; and, though the result was not a model piece of editing, the intensive study of Glinka's beautifully transparent scoring and simple, natural part-writing reawakened and even deepened Rimsky-Korsakov's old passion for the composer of *Ruslan* and led him back from the early eighteenth century to the nineteenth. Balakirev may have been an 'altogether changed man' in some respects, but his character was in no way changed. He at once adopted his old attitude of mentor to Rimsky-Korsakov, and at first the other meekly gave way 'from old habit and from my submissive nature'. Balakirev censured Korsakov for entering the chamber music competition, began to meddle in the affairs of the Free School and the constitution of its concert programmes, and interfered in Rimsky-Korsakov's revision of his *Maid of Pskov*. Before long their relations became badly strained.

The colossal task of rewriting his opera, which occupied Rimsky-Korsakov from the autumn of 1876 until January, 1878, originated with the idea of adding a prologue based on the First Act of Mey's play (which had been cut out of the first version), and in the composer's dissatisfaction with the 'harmonic exaggerations', the 'absence of a contrapuntal element' and the orchestration of the opera in its original form. Now Balakirev demanded the insertion in Act IV of a chorus of begging pilgrims, based on the song of 'Alexey the Man of God' (from the Filippov collection of folk-songs), not because begging pilgrims had anything to do with the action, but simply because he liked the tune; Korsakov himself thought it would be nice to introduce a 'Royal hunt and storm' like Berlioz's in *Les Troyens*; and in this absurdly childish spirit he proceeded to recast the work, entirely ruining it by the forcible introduction of quite uncalled-for 'contrapuntal interest', though, curiously enough, he still avoided the use of valve-horns and trumpets in the reorchestration. On the whole the new version pleased no one, neither his friends nor his wife nor himself. He had got rid of the amateurish crudities and turned *The Maid* into a respectable, professorial opera but—'I felt myself that it was long, dry and heavy'. He made a half-hearted attempt to get the new version produced and was annoyed, rather than discouraged, by its failure. 'I felt it was all for the best' and that, at any rate, 'my course of education was finished', though he still wrote a few more rather academic piano pieces, Opp. 10 and 11. The 'chorus of begging pilgrims' was almost immediately published separately as Op. 20, while the composer made an orchestral suite of *Music to Mey's Drama, 'The Maid of Pskov'*, from the new miniature overture to the Prologue, two of the entr'actes and two newly composed entr'actes based on material from the main part of the opera.

Even while still engaged on this unlucky second version of *The Maid*, during the summer of 1877, Rimsky-Korsakov's thoughts had been turning more and more often to his wife's cherished idea of an opera based on Gogol's *May Night*, and he actually began it in February, 1878—with the

Third Act. He wrote the full score at once, sometimes working far into the night. The composition went so quickly and easily that by the end of April not only the bulk of the Third Act but two numbers of the First were finished and could be played to Mussorgsky, Cui, Stassov and the young Lyadov. They must have felt that Korsakov was himself again, for everything in *May Night* is lyrical or humorous and delicately coloured, shot through with folk-song and with scoring frankly modelled on Glinka's (even with natural brass still). Of counterpoint for counterpoint's sake there is hardly a trace. However, Rimsky-Korsakov had an opportunity to gratify his love of 'musical tricks' that spring and summer in the famous *Paraphrases* in which he collaborated with Borodin, Cui and Lyadov. Indeed, he was so much more industrious than the rest that some of his pieces—a sonatina, a chorale ('Eine feste Burg'), a 'recitative *alla Bach*' and others—had to be omitted from the printed edition.

The R.M.S. had organized several concerts of Russian music in Paris in connexion with the World Exhibition during the summer of 1878, and it was proposed to send Rimsky-Korsakov, incompetent conductor as he was, to direct them. He regarded the matter as quite settled when, fortunately for the credit of Russian music, it was decided to send Nicholas Rubinstein instead. There was a storm, and for a time Rimsky-Korsakov avoided Rubinstein during the latter's visits to Petersburg. The composition of *May Night* proceeded smoothly at the summer-villa at Ligovo, being interrupted only by a few duty

visits to Kronstadt and by the birth of a second
son, Andrey. The full score was finished, all but
the overture, in October. (It seems that, in
spite of Rimsky-Korsakov's statement in his
memoirs, the overture was not written till the
following summer.) The vocal score was finished
that winter; the work was at once accepted by
the Theatre Directorate; and the choral rehearsals
began in the spring of 1879. Even before this,
three choruses from the new opera had been
performed at the Free School concerts.

From lack of money the School had given
no public concerts the previous season, but in
January and February of 1879 Rimsky-Korsakov
conducted four. They are important landmarks
in the history of Russian music, for in addition to
the *May Night* pieces they included first performances of Borodin's Polovtsian Dances and two
other numbers from *Prince Igor*, hurriedly orchestrated specially for these concerts, and of the
'Pimen's cell' scene from *Boris*. At the fourth
concert there was a disaster in a Liszt concerto,
caused by a nervous pianist. 'I literally wept
for shame', Korsakov confessed, 'when I reached
home after the concert'. Nevertheless we find
him, undismayed, conducting a couple of concerts
in Moscow for the pianist Shostakovsky a month
or two later.

That summer, again spent at Ligovo, the
composer wrote a string quartet entirely based on
Russian folk-tunes, the movements being entitled
respectively 'In the Fields', 'In the Maidens'
Room', 'Khorovod' and 'At the Monastery'. It
was tried through by the 'cellist K. Y. Davidov,

E

who had succeeded Azanchevsky as Director of
the Conservatoire in 1876, and his quartet. But
the work displeased the composer and it was never
publicly performed though, as we shall see, none
of the material was wasted. He also took with
him to Ligovo another scene from *Igor*, intending
to 'revise', complete, and score it—in postal
consultation with Borodin. But Borodin, who
had accepted his friend's pressing offer of assistance only with reluctance, made it clear that he
did not care for the idea, and nothing came of it.
Before returning to Petersburg Korsakov began
'an orchestral piece of fantastic character on
Pushkin's Prologue to *Ruslan and Lyudmila*'.
The Prologue enumerates all the characteristic
figures of Russian folk-lore and it appears from
a letter to his friend the Moscow critic, S. N.
Kruglikov, that the composer intended to name it
after one of the most striking of these figures: 'I've
done nothing during the summer'. (Evidently
the quartet counted as 'nothing'.) 'Only begun
a musical picture *Baba Yaga*, but it's not going very
well and I don't know whether I shall go on with
it yet for a while'. Balakirev also disapproving
of the fragment, Korsakov laid it aside and
instead set about the revision and reorchestration
of his early *Overture on Three Russian Themes*, which
occupied his spare time throughout the winter.

Of 'spare' time he really had very little, for in
addition to his official duties there were four Free
School concerts to prepare—with Balakirev butting
in at rehearsals and, much to his annoyance,
publicly teaching him how to conduct; he had to
orchestrate Mussorgsky's 'Persian Dances' from

Khovanshchina so that they should be ready in time for the concert (and he characteristically took the opportunity 'to correct a great deal of the harmony and part-writing'); there were the administrative affairs of the Free School to attend to; and the rehearsals of *May Night* having begun in October he had to be present to accompany the soloists. Orchestral rehearsals of his opera began in the middle of December (just a week before the fourteen-year-old Glazunov came for his first lesson) and the first performance took place, after several postponements, on January 9th/21st, 1880. Napravnik conducted, F. P. Komissarzhevsky (father of the famous actor and producer) sang Levko, and F. I. Stravinsky (father of Igor Stravinsky) took the part of the Headman. It was a success but by no means a triumph. Two numbers were encored and the opera was repeated seven times more before the end of the season, but after a year or so it was withdrawn from the current repertoire.[1]

But Rimsky-Korsakov was already pressing ahead with a third opera. As early as 1874 he had read Ostrovsky's charming play, *Snow Maiden*, for which Tchaïkovsky had supplied the incidental music, but had not been impressed by it. It had struck him as too fantastic. 'Why? Were the idaes of the sixties still alive in me, or was I in the grip of the fashion of the seventies

---

[1] From this period (January, 1880) dates Korsakov's contribution to the music for an abortive series of 'living pictures' intended to commemorate the twenty-fifth anniversary of the accession of Alexander II: a piece *Slava* for chorus and orchestra, Op. 21, furbished up from an old fugal exercise of 1876 on the well-known folk-song used in the coronation scene of *Boris* and in Korsakov's own *Overture on Three Russian Themes*.

for "subjects taken from *life*"? Or was I caught in
the stream of Mussorgsky's naturalism? Probably
all three'. But now, reading it again in February,
1880, his eyes were opened to its 'marvellous
poetic beauty'. 'I at once wanted to write an
opera on this subject, and the more I thought
about it the deeper I fell in love with Ostrovsky's
legend. My mild interest in the ancient Russian
customs and heathen pantheism flamed up.
There seemed no better subject in the whole
world than this, no more poetic figures than Snow
Maiden, Lel or the Spring Fairy, no better realm
than the kingdom of the Berendeys with their
marvellous Tsar, no better religion and philosophy
of life than the worship of the Sun God, Yarilo'.
He at once sketched out the final sun-worshipping
chorus. 'My head was immediately thronged with
motives, themes and chord-progressions, and the
moods and colours of the different moments of the
action presented themselves to my imagination,
first elusively, then more and more clearly'. All
these fragments were noted down in 'a fat book
of music-paper'. Visiting Moscow in April to
conduct a concert, the composer took the opportunity to call on Ostrovsky himself and get his
permission to adapt his play. The dramatist
willingly granted it, gave him a copy of the play,
and later expressed not only his delight in
Korsakov's 'wonderful music' but his approval
of Korsakov's libretto. 'I have found very few
verses which, in my opinion, need revision', he
wrote to the composer in November.

That summer the Rimsky-Korsakovs found a
new summer residence on the Stelëvo estate;

twenty miles from Luga. 'The house, though old, was comfortable; it had a lovely great shady garden with fruit-trees'. They arrived on May 18th/30th. 'For the first time in my life I spent the summer in the heart of the Russian country-side. Everything delighted me. The beautiful position, the delightful woods, the great forest or Volchinets, the fields of rye, buckwheat, oats, flax, and millet, the host of scattered trees, the little stream where we bathed, the nearness of the great Lake Vrevo, the isolated villages with their ancient Russian names—all this enchanted me. The lovely garden with its multitude of cherry- and apple-trees, currant-bushes, strawberries, gooseberries, with its flowering lilacs, its host of wild-flowers and the ceaseless singing of the birds— all this peculiarly harmonized with my pantheistic feeling at the time and with my delight in the subject of *Snow Maiden*. Some thick and twisted bough or tree - stump, overgrown with moss, would seem to me the Wood Spirit or his dwelling; the forest of Volchinets, the forbidden forest of the tale; the summit of Mount Kopïtets, Yarilo's mountain; the threefold echo which we heard from our balcony—the voices of the wood spirits'. And years afterwards Rimsky-Korsakov confessed to Yastrebtsev that at that period he actually 'began to *pray to nature*—to a crooked old tree-stump, to some willow or century-old oak, to the forest stream, to the lake, even to a great head of cabbage, to a black ram or at the cockcrow scattering the sorcery of the night. In all these things I saw something peculiar and supernatural. It sometimes seemed to me that animals, birds, and even trees and flowers, know more of the magic and fantastic than human beings do; that they understand the language of nature far better! You will say that all this was fearfully exaggerated and illogical, and yet it seemed to me that it was all really so! I warmly believed in it all, as a child would, like a dreamer surrendering himself to his fancies, and yet, strangely enough, in those minutes the world seemed to me nearer, more understandable, and I was somehow merged with it! And even now'—that was in 1894—'when the period of the summer solstice has lost some of its old significance for me, I still can't altogether renounce every kind of pantheistic idea'. We must remember that pantheism was very much in the air in Russia at that period. Chekhov was a pantheist and, according to Merezhkovsky, the great majority of cultured Russians were toying with some variety or other of pantheism.

In that extraordinary state of mind Rimsky-Korsakov 'composed all day and every day' all through the hot and thundery summer, though he found time to help his wife make jam and find mushrooms. With nothing but a cracked old piano, a whole tone flat (so that he called it his 'piano in B flat'), to try over what he had composed, he began writing directly in the full score as he had done with *May Night*. But his thoughts ran far ahead of his fingers and he was obliged to content himself with making an ordinary vocal score. The whole opera, one of his most delightful works, was finished in this form on August 12th/24th. Nor was it his only work that summer, as appears from a letter .to Kruglikov (July 21st/

August 2nd): 'I've sketched out the whole of my *Legend* in score; it only remains to put the finishing touches, i.e. to add a bit here and there in the *tuttis*. Have also roughed out the instrumentation of my Russian quartet, turning it into a sinfonietta'. The *Legend* in question was the orchestral piece, Op. 29, begun the summer before and originally called *Baba Yaga*, while the 'Russian quartet' was, of course, the one based on folk-tunes. Korsakov completed the *Legend* before returning to Petersburg in September, but the Sinfonietta, Op. 31, consisting of the first three movements of the quartet, drastically revised as well as orchestrated, was laid aside and not completed till the summer of 1884. (The material of the fourth movement of the quartet was used years afterwards in the opera *Sadko*.) Rimsky-Korsakov at once set to work at the orchestration of *Snow Maiden*, this time writing for chromatic brass, beginning it on September 7th/19th and finishing the six-hundred-page score on March 26th/April 7th, 1881. Having completed it, he felt himself 'a mature musician, standing firmly on my feet as an opera composer'. To Kruglikov he expressed his view of his own position in relation to his friends with characteristic candour: 'Owing to deficient technique Balakirev writes little, Borodin slowly, Cui perfunctorily, Mussorgsky untidily and often nonsensically. Don't imagine that I've altered my opinion of their compositions. If only these people had good, sound technique, what mightn't they do! Although I'm perfectly sincere in saying that I consider them far more talented than myself, I don't envy them a straw'.

In January, 1881, Rimsky-Korsakov conducted his new *Legend* at an R.M.S. concert; in February, the first Free School concert of the season. Three others had been advertised, but the assassination of Alexander II, at the beginning of March, put an end to all concert-giving. Mussorgsky, who had appeared to take the applause for his *Destruction of Sennacherib* at the Free School concert, was taken ill shortly afterwards and died a fortnight after the Tsar, and Rimsky-Korsakov undertook the colossal task of preparing his dead friend's works for publication. The labour was an unselfish one and occupied nearly two years of valuable time, no mean sacrifice, and it is infinitely regrettable that, owing to the pedantic spirit in which he carried it out, it has earned him more abuse than gratitude. Perhaps his own excuse is the best: 'If Mussorgsky's compositions are fated to last unfaded for fifty years after his death, then an archæologically exact edition can be issued' (which is exactly what has happened). 'In the meantime what was needed was an edition for performance, for practical artistic purposes, for the making known of his great talent, not for the study of his personality and artistic transgressions'.

In June Korsakov went to Nikolaev again to inspect the bands of the Black Sea Fleet, and conduct them in an open-air concert. 'I've been doling out thanks and praise', he wrote to Nadezhda, 'and generally playing the Khlestakov' —the comic hero of Gogol's *Revizor*—'a stupid rôle that doesn't suit me a bit. I never know how to carry it out with the proper solemnity and importance'. His duty finished, he was joined by

Nadezhda for a holiday trip in the Crimea. At
the hotel at Yalta, run by Stassov's son-in-law,
they met a number of old acquaintances, including
Korsakov's old commander, Zeleny of the *Almaz*,
and made a new one, the young Felix Blumenfeld.
From Yalta they went on to Sevastopol and thence
to Constantinople for three days, returning home
by way of Odessa and Kiev, and spending the
rest of the summer with the children at Taitsa.

For at least a year Rimsky-Korsakov had been
anxious to wash his hands of the Free School,
which was constantly in financial difficulties and
which occupied a great deal of time to little
purpose. The choir had too many bad voices;
the women were all too old; there were very few
good men; the tenors were woolly. And so on,
and so on. In short, the Free School choir was
like almost every other amateur choir that has
ever existed in any country. All that induced
him to persevere was the opportunity it gave him
of performing whatever he liked—and the fact
that he saw no alternative to himself, except
Lyadov, who was not energetic enough, and not
yet well enough known. It now seemed to him
that as Balakirev was once more taking an active
interest in the School the original Director might
as well resume his post. Accordingly, he resigned
in September and Balakirev, after a show of
hesitation, accepted the committee's invitation and
again took over the direction. In his memoirs,
which are marked throughout by an unpleasant
tone of hostility towards Balakirev, Rimsky-
Korsakov gives a rather different account of this
episode. He says that 'Balakirev's constant

interference in the affairs of the School became
intolerable for me'. But his correspondence shows
that that was quite a secondary reason. He
frankly told Kruglikov at the time that Balakirev
was 'a thousand times more suited to the position
than I'.

Rimsky-Korsakov's immediate task was the
editing and scoring of Mussorgsky's *Khovanshchina*;
the last act, with which he began, was completed
and orchestrated by December. And in the meantime, rehearsals of his own *Snow Maiden* were going
ahead. Nadezhda, although pregnant, insisted
on being present at them, and actually gave birth
to a son (Volodya) just after attending one of the
last. In consequence, she was unable to attend
the first performance on January 29th/February
10th, 1882, and her husband, much distraught and
(it appears) slightly intoxicated, hung about
behind the scenes in a state of profound gloom,
hearing practically nothing of his music. Like
May Night, the new opera had reasonable success
and a bad press, even from Cui.

The Third Act of *Khovanshchina* was finished in
May, the First and Second at Stelëvo during the
summer, the Fourth after Korsakov's return to
St. Petersburg. The *Night on the Bare Mountain* at
first defeated his efforts to make a 'practical
edition' of it, but Mussorgsky's other smaller
works were soon polished up and at once published
by Bessel. A reorchestration, with chromatic
brass, of his own suite from the second version of
The Maid of Pskov also dates from this period.

The stay at Stelëvo was interrupted in August
by a fortnight's visit to Moscow for the All-Russian

Art and Industrial Exhibition, a visit which had
unexpectedly important consequences. Korsakov,
who had been invited to conduct a couple of
concerts, had included in one of his programmes
the sixteen - year - old Sasha Glazunov's First
Symphony. 'Before the first rehearsal of the Symphony, a tall, handsome man came up to me . . .
introduced himself as Mitrofan Petrovich Belaev
and asked permission to attend all the rehearsals.
Belaev, a passionate lover of music, had been so
completely enraptured by Glazunov's Symphony
at its first performance at the Free School' (in
March, under Balakirev) 'that he had come to
Moscow specially to hear it again'. The meeting
of Rimsky-Korsakov and Belaev in 1882 is a
milestone in the history of Russian music.

The orchestration of *Khovanshchina* being practic-
cally completed,[1] Rimsky-Korsakov again found
time for original composition. His Piano Concerto, a one-movement work based on a Russian
theme, was finished on January 3rd/15th, 1883.
But he was on the eve of a fresh appointment,
which, at first, allowed him little time for creative
work.

Among the wholesale changes consequent on
the accession of Alexander III, the long reign of
the seventy-six-year-old Bakhmetev as Intendant
of the Imperial Chapel at last came to an end.
(He had been Intendant since 1861). But his
successor, Count Sheremetev, was not even an
amateur musician, and it became necessary to

[1] The opera was rejected by a majority vote of the opera
committee in April, and more than a quarter of a century was to
pass before Mussorgsky's second opera was given on the Imperial
stage.

revive the post of Musical Director. Thanks to the wire-pulling of Filippov, who had great influence both in Government circles and with the Holy Synod, Balakirev was, in February, 1883, appointed to the Directorship, with Rimsky-Korsakov as his assistant. In May the entire Chapel were obliged to spend three weeks in Moscow for the coronation ceremonies and, although his family moved to Taitsa for the summer, the journeys to the Chapel at Old Peterhof twice a week left Korsakov little time for the composition of anything but a little church music. In November he writes: 'I'm very busy with the Chapel and not writing anything. Nor do I want to. It seems to me that I've written a full stop after *Snow Maiden*, and that the songs, Concerto and religious music are only in the nature of reminiscences of days long past. My head at the moment is simply a Torricellian vacuum'. Rimsky-Korsakov was at first genuinely interested in his new work and, in view of his expanding family, was no doubt glad of the additional salary (2300 rubles a year); at any rate he had moved into a bigger town house in the autumn. (In September, 1889, he was given quarters in the new official buildings of the Chapel.) On the other hand, he lost his other official post in March, 1884. Krabbe had been supplanted by a new Minister of Marine who, in the interests of economy, abolished the Inspectorship of Naval Bands. And already in January, in less than a year, Korsakov began to find his new duties 'boring and dry'. 'I'm writing nothing', he tells Kruglikov again.

In every way Rimsky-Korsakov's life was changing. The old circle of friends was loosening. Mussorgsky was dead; he saw little of Cui; Balakirev now moved mostly in a new circle of his own, a coterie pious rather than musical. Of the old band, only Borodin and Stassov were still frequent visitors at the Rimsky-Korsakovs'. Instead there were new faces, mostly ex-pupils who were now on the footing of friends—Lyadov, Glazunov, Blumenfeld, Ippolitov-Ivanov and Arensky—trained musicians very different in outlook from the hot-headed young amateurs who had banded together in the early sixties. And now this circle found a new focus in the house of the Mæcenas, M. P. Belaev, a curious character: hater of women, masterful, hospitable, good-hearted, brutally frank. Belaev, himself an amateur viola-player, was passionately fond of chamber music, and every Friday the circle gathered at his house to play and hear string quartets. At 1 A.M. they would adjourn to supper; after that Glazunov or one of the other young men would play through some new composition. They seldom broke up till three in the morning, and even then Belaev would carry off some of the livelier members to continue the festivity at a restaurant—a practice of which the temperate and strictly moral Rimsky-Korsakov strongly disapproved. In this atmosphere the younger composers were naturally encouraged to write, bring and try out chamber music—especially as Belaev made it a practice to 'christen' every new work generously with champagne. The immediate result was an extraordinary crop of Russian quartet music, mostly of a rather light kind, which Belaev himself launched into publicity.

Having had Glazunov's First Symphony printed at his own expense, in score, parts and piano-duet arrangement, by the Leipzig firm of Röder, he began to issue the works of his other new friends in the same manner, and so found himself embarked on a career as a music-publisher. In the same lavish way, in March, 1884, he hired a hall and the Opera orchestra for a private rehearsal of some of Glazunov's works; in November, 1885, financed a public concert of Russian orchestral music; and in 1886 founded a regular series of concerts, the 'Russian Symphony Concerts'. Rimsky - Korsakov was, naturally, at Belaev's elbow as his adviser in all these matters, and a large batch of his works, early and later, was at once published by the new firm, with opus-numbers in very misleading sequence. Cui, it may be mentioned, had very little connexion with the Belaev circle; Balakirev, none at all.

All this time Rimsky-Korsakov remained quite unproductive, though busily engaged in wiping out the sins of his musical past. In March, 1884, a day or two after the above-mentioned private performance of Glazunov's First Symphony, he took out the score of his own 'naïve and youthful' First Symphony. It seemed to him that, brushed up, it might be of use to amateur orchestras, and he spent the early part of the summer in revising and reorchestrating it. Among other changes he transposed it up a semitone to E minor and altered the sequence of movements, putting the *andante* before the scherzo. In this form it at last got into print, being published by Bessel. For the rest he finished the orchestration of the Sinfonietta and in August began the scherzo of a Fourth Symphony. But this came to nothing after only four days' work, and the composer devoted the rest of the summer and autumn to the writing of a harmony text-book, primarily for the use of his young students, the lads of the Imperial Chapel, whose musical education was in his hands. At this period he was completely in the rut of administrative routine, and he declined even to change one rut for another when Tchaïkovsky, in April, 1885, sounded him as to his willingness to accept the Directorship of the Moscow Conservatoire.

The summer of 1885 passed just as unproductively at Taitsa and in visits to the Chapel at Peterhof. Still living in his musical past, he now began to brood over his unlucky Third Symphony, and revised and re-scored the first movement. A melancholy change from the white-hot inspiration of the summer of 1880 at Stelëvo! Nor did a two-months' holiday in the Caucasus with Nadezhda in the summer of 1886 reawaken his creative impulse. The lovely scenery around the Caucasian spas inspired him to nothing but the rewriting of the third movement of the Third Symphony. Pyatigorsk, Tiflis, the steamer trip to Batum, Yalta and Simferopol in the Crimea, all gave him delightful memories, but nothing more. He went back to Taitsa with no other idea than the futile attempt to breathe life into the dry bones of the Symphony, a labour accomplished without much success soon after his return to Petersburg in

September. He did break his long silence that winter with the first movement of the *B-la-F* Quartet, in which he collaborated with Borodin, Lyadov and Glazunov in celebrating Belaev's name-day in November. But the movement is hardly one of his most masterly compositions. Nor did the *Fantasia on Russian Themes* for violin and orchestra, written for Krasnokutsky, the violin teacher of the Imperial Chapel, suggest that the composer was on the eve of a fresh burst of creative activity. Though the themes are attractive, their treatment is of slight interest, the orchestral part being very evidently written for the pupils' orchestra of the Chapel. Yet the piece was to have a most brilliant sequel.

CHAPTER VI

1887–93

Death of Borodin – Rimsky-Korsakov and Glazunov complete
Prince Igor – the *Spanish Capriccio* – *Jour de Fête* Quartet – *Easter
Overture* and *Sheherazade* – Wagner's influence – *Mlada* –
Rimsky-Korsakov conducts at the Paris Exhibition – French
musicians – in Brussels – family misfortunes – third version of
The Maid of Pskov – 'no use for music' – 'a great part of the
Russian school is cold, brain-spun stuff' – strained relations
with Balakirev – typically Russian crisis – preoccupation with
æsthetics and philosophy – alarming physical phenomena –
lapses of memory – dislike of the Imperial Chapel – Masha's
illness and death at Yalta.

IN February, 1887, almost the last link between
Rimsky-Korsakov's past and his present was
broken by the death of Borodin. It is recorded
that he spent a sleepless night when he heard the
news. Only four months before (October 15th/
27th), at the very first of the new 'Russian
Symphony Concerts' financed by Belaev, Rimsky-
Korsakov had conducted his version of Mussorgsky's *Night on the Bare Mountain* and so closed his
account, as he thought, with one dead friend.
Now it fell to him to carry out the same duty for
another. Above all, there was *Prince Igor* to be
finished and orchestrated. 'Well, now there will
be an end to *Igor*', someone had said when
Borodin died. And Rimsky-Korsakov, hearing the
remark, determined to make it true in a sense not
thought of by the speaker. With Glazunov he
set about the work in the spring, and it went ahead
by leaps and bounds during the summer, un-
interrupted even by the duty visits to the Chapel

at Peterhof—for Glazunov happened to be spending the summer there, and they had plenty of
opportunities for consultation. Instead of Taitsa,
the Rimsky-Korsakovs had taken a new villa at
Nikolskoe, on Lake Nelay, and the air must have
worked beneficially on the composer's dormant
faculties for he took up the sketches for a violin
fantasia on Spanish themes, which he had thought
of writing as a companion-piece to his Russian
fantasia, and used them instead for a purely
orchestral work, the famous *Spanish Capriccio*, a
piece of virtuoso orchestral writing which seems
to glitter with all the power and brilliance
accumulated during the six years of almost
complete silence since *Snow Maiden*. That the
orchestral effect of the *Capriccio* is the 'very essence
of the composition, not its mere dressing-up',
the composer was careful to insist himself. The
Capriccio completed on July 23rd/August 4th,
Rimsky-Korsakov returned to the orchestration
of *Igor* and, incidentally, wrote another chapter of
the memoirs tentatively begun eleven years before.

That year only three composers collaborated in
the quartet for Belaev's name-day (*Jour de Fête*),
Korsakov contributing the finale. But the dead
comrade was commemorated in the first Russian
Symphony Concert of the season, which was
entirely devoted to Borodin's compositions. At
the fifth concert, December 5th/17th, Rimsky-
Korsakov conducted the first performance of the
Spanish Capriccio, which was received with such
enthusiasm that it had to be repeated. The first
rehearsal had been interrupted again and again
by the applause of the orchestra, and the composer

gracefully returned thanks by dedicating the work
to them. The *Capriccio* was immediately followed
by two other orchestral works of the same exceptionally brilliant type—the *Easter Overture* and
Sheherazade, both sketched in Petersburg in the
early months of 1888 and, as usual, completed
in the country (this year at Nezhgovitsĭ, some
twelve miles from Luga). *Sheherazade* was finished
on July 26th/August 7th, almost exactly a year
after the completion of the *Capriccio*. These three
compositions, Korsakov considered, 'close a period
of my work, at the end of which my orchestration
had attained a considerable degree of virtuosity
and warm sonority without Wagnerian influence,
limiting myself to the normally constituted
orchestra used by Glinka'.

But Rimsky-Korsakov was no longer to live in
virginal innocence and almost complete ignorance
of the mature Wagner. That very winter
Neumann's Travelling Opera Company visited
Petersburg and gave the whole of the *Ring* for the
first time in Russia, at the Maryinsky Theatre,
Karl Muck conducting. Korsakov and Glazunov
attended every rehearsal, following from the score.
'Wagner's handling of the orchestra astonished
both of us', says Rimsky-Korsakov, 'and from
this time onward Wagner's methods gradually
permeated our orchestral writing'. It is strange
that a composer of forty-four who had just written
three such masterpieces of orchestration as the
Capriccio, the *Easter Overture* and *Sheherazade* should
have been so ready to pick up someone else's
tricks. Actually, the first fruit of Wagner's
influence on Korsakov was his orchestration of the

polonaise from *Boris*, which he considered Mussorg-sky had scored very ineffectively. The conduct-ing of all six of the Russian Symphony Concerts that winter—*Sheherazade* and the *Easter Overture* both being given for the first time on December 3rd/15th—left Rimsky-Korsakov little leisure for original composition, but he reorchestrated his early *Serbian Fantasia* and in January actually began to tinker again at his *Maid of Pskov*. But a trifling incident sent his thoughts off at a fresh angle.

On the second anniversary of Borodin's death (that is, on February 15th/27th, 1889) a party of friends—Stassov, Glazunov, Lyadov, Belaev and the Rimsky-Korsakovs—gathered at his old house 'to spend the evening together in memory of the dear fellow'. Among other of his manuscripts which they played over and discussed was that of the finale of the Fourth Act he had contributed to the collective *Mlada*, which Korsakov now made up his mind to orchestrate. 'In the middle of our conversation and our reminiscences of Borodin, Lyadov all of a sudden remarked that *Mlada* would make a suitable subject for me. Without hesita-tion, I replied, "Very well, I'll get on with it at once"'. To Stassov's great delight, the subject completely captured his fancy. He determined to rewrite the original unsatisfactory libretto himself and to lay the music out on the most generous scale, with full Wagnerian orchestra. The revision of *The Maid of Pskov* was postponed indefinitely; ideas for *Mlada* began to accumulate.

The composition of the new opera was inter-rupted in the summer by a visit to Paris for the

World Exhibition. Belaev was financing two symphony concerts of Russian music by the Colonne Orchestra in the Palais du Trocadéro and Rimsky-Korsakov was to conduct both. Sending the children with his mother to Nezhgovitsï, he and Nadezhda set out with Belaev, Glazunov and the pianist Lavrov. The concerts were successful from an artistic point of view, but as Belaev, with truly Russian philosophy, had done very little to advertise them, on the ground that those who were really interested were bound to find out about them in any case, the audiences were very poor. Rimsky-Korsakov was no lover of the Parisians, and he has left us some caustic impressions of an official dinner 'after which a repulsively fat old operetta singer sang' and of some of the musicians with whom he came in contact. 'Delibes gave me the impression of a simple, amiable man, Massenet—that of an artful fox; Augusta Holmes was a very *décolletée* person; Messager struck me as rather colourless . . . ' and so on. From the playing of panpipes in a Hungarian band and the music accompanying the Algerian dancing girls at the Exhibition, he took one or two hints for *Mlada*. But when the concerts were over the Rimsky-Korsakovs left their companions as soon as possible and made an excursion to Switzerland and the Salzkammergut, returning by way of Vienna. In July they rejoined the children at Nezhgovitsï, where the composition of *Mlada* proceeded at such a rate that on August 31st/September 12th, Rimsky-Korsakov could report to Kruglikov: 'Lyadov gave me the idea of writing *Mlada* on February

15th and on August 15th I wrote the last note of the draft; in other words, all this has taken just six months, to say nothing of a month and a half spent over the examinations, a month of travelling abroad and two weeks spent in making the duet arrangement of *Sheherazade*'. (He notes in his memoirs that 'the Wagnerian system of leitmotives considerably hastened the process of composition'.) On the other hand the scoring for an exceptionally large orchestra was to take unusually long and was moreover subjected to all sorts of interruptions.

In April, 1890, Rimsky-Korsakov was invited to go to Brussels to conduct a concert of Russian music in the Théâtre de la Monnaie. Belgium was just then at the height of her enthusiasm for Russian music, excited by the visits of Borodin and Cui, and Rimsky-Korsakov was fêted and made much of by the leading Belgian musicians, who appear to have impressed him much more favourably than the Parisian ones. But he returned from Brussels to find Nadezhda dangerously ill with diphtheria; and Andrey soon caught the infection. 'Everything in the flat is turned upside-down', he writes in May. 'The children have been sent away to different houses; I've had to arrange for them to be sent into the country as soon as possible. . . . The present year has been very unlucky for me; I've had nothing but dangers and commotion, and all this has descended on my unfortunate *Mlada*, which will probably be my last composition . . . (at any rate, the last important one)'. In the summer they all, with his eighty-seven-year-old mother, moved as usual to Nezhgovitsï, where he found

time to orchestrate Borodin's *Mlada* finale, besides
working at his own opera. But in August his
mother fell ill, and had to be taken to Petersburg,
where she died on the 31st/September 12th.
However, three days later the composer was able
to inform Kruglikov that 'I finished the orchestral
score of *Mlada* some days ago'. But the same ill-
fortune pursued him till the end of the year. The
first performance of *Igor* in October brought him
much satisfaction. But the festivities, including
a concert, with which his friends and pupils
celebrated the twenty-fifth anniversary of his
career as a composer in December (reckoning
from the performance of his First Symphony)
were streaked with unpleasantness owing to a
squabble with Balakirev, who curtly refused to
attend the official lunch. The same month the
Rimsky-Korsakovs lost their baby Slavchik, and
the second youngest child, the two-year-old
Masha, fell ill directly afterwards.

In February, 1891, the Third Act of *Mlada* was
given a concert performance at one of Belaev's
concerts and the work was accepted by the Theatre
Directorate. That disposed of, Korsakov again
returned to the revision of *The Maid of Pskov*, dis-
carding the second version as a whole and basing
this third and final version mainly on the first.
He also entirely re-scored it, the bulk of the work
being done between April, 1891, and April, 1892.
With yet another revision made in 1891, a fresh
orchestration of *Sadko*, 'I closed my account with
my past. Not one of my major works *of the period
before "May Night"* remained in its original form'.
But nothing new came from him. The outburst

which had produced the three big orchestral works and *Mlada* seemed to have exhausted itself. It really looked as if *Mlada* were going to be his 'last important work', though it is true he was thinking of an opera on the *Sadko* subject or perhaps one on a play of Mey's—*Servilia* or *The Tsar's Bride*. He actually began some sketches for a *Zoryushka*, an opera-project abandoned by Lyadov, but they came to nothing.

The Rimsky-Korsakovs spent the summer of 1891 in Switzerland, vainly hoping the change would do little Masha good. Nicholas was too disturbed to work; even a little scoring which he began turned out badly. Two letters written that August bear witness to his profound pessimism and sense of disillusionment at this period. 'While I was abroad, it seemed to me that music didn't grip and satisfy me; and now, it appears, I have no use for it at all'. A week later he found the new compositions of his nearest and dearest young friends 'boring . . . paltry and worthless . . . dry and lifeless'. 'In short, pretty harmonies and the interweaving of melodious phrases don't affect me at all; it all seems to me cold and dry. *Mlada* is as cold as ice. Now a Beethoven quartet or symphony is another matter. Technique and working out are there only the outward form, and everything is filled with life and soul. . . . I fancy that a great part of the Russian School is not music, but cold, brain-spun stuff. . . . Having such thoughts, I ought to leave off composing. . . . Don't regret that I've torn up the book I was writing, in a fit of stupid bitterness, and that I can't remember what I'd written. None of it was worth a farthing'. (What this 'book' was remains unknown.) Autumn, spring and winter passed in the same way. The third version of *The Maid* progressed slowly; Korsakov amused himself in the winter by orchestrating the coronation scene from *Boris* according to his own ideas; relations with Balakirev became more and more strained. There are some curious and contradictory phrases in a letter of April, 1892: 'I teach and learn, teach and learn, am vexed by many things and cultivate an objective outlook. I nurse within myself a feeling of extreme repugnance towards Balakirev—(and with success)'.

The summer at Nezhgovitsï was one of real crisis, a crisis of a nature partly physical, partly intellectual, curiously similar to those which have overcome so many Russian artists in mid-career, in which they lose themselves and change the course of their lives. (For instance, Gogol, Tolstoy and Balakirev.[1]) At first Korsakov worked for three or four weeks at the new version of the Overture to *The Maid of Pskov*, but 'with extraordinary reluctance, feeling a sort of weariness and disgust'. That finished, he thought of writing an essay or even a book on Russian music, particularly his own compositions, Borodin's and Mussorgsky's. There was to be an introduction dealing with æsthetics in general, which would lead to musical æsthetics in particular and this in turn to the Russian School. It was quickly written—and as quickly destroyed as hopelessly

[1] See an article by the present writer in *The Contemporary Review* for November, 1933, reprinted in the book *On Russian Music* (William Reeves, 1939).

inadequate, like the book begun the previous summer. Rimsky-Korsakov began to read books on musical æsthetics—Ambros and Hanslick—and La Mara's biographies of the great composers. Hanslick annoyed him but sent him back with fresh energy to his own book. But the more he wrote, the bigger grew his plan and the more conscious he became of his ignorance of æsthetics and philosophy in general. He broke off his work to study G. H. Lewes's *Biographical History of Philosophy*, but in the intervals of reading wrote short studies of 'Mozart and Glinka'[1] and similar subjects, only to condemn them as 'unripe'. Lewes filled his head only with a mass of disconnected thoughts, and he sat 'for whole days' while they turned over and over in his mind. 'Then one fine morning at the end of August or beginning of September, I felt extreme weariness, accompanied by a rush of blood to the head and complete confusion of my thoughts. I was seriously alarmed and on the very first day completely lost my appetite. When I told my wife about this she naturally persuaded me to stop all work, which I did until we returned to Petersburg, read nothing, walked all day, endeavouring not to be left alone. When I was left alone certain unpleasant fixed ideas thrust themselves importunately into my head. I thought about religion and a humble reconciliation with Balakirev. However, the walks and rest helped, and by the time I returned to Petersburg I had got myself completely under control. But to music I was

[1] These fragments were published posthumously with his other prose-writings. They are of very moderate interest.

completely indifferent, and the thought of pursuing my philosophical studies constantly haunted me. In spite of the doctor's advice, I began to read a lot—a textbook of logic, the philosophies of Herbert Spencer and Spinoza, the æsthetic writings of Guyau, various histories of philosophy, etc. Almost every day I bought new books and read them, skipping from one to another, scribbling marginal notes, thinking and thinking and making notes. I wanted to write a great work on the æsthetics of musical art. For the time being I put the Russian School on one side. But instead of æsthetics I got involved in metaphysics in general, fearing to begin in too shallow a way. And then the very unpleasant phenomena began to reappear more and more frequently in my head; not so much rushes of blood to the head or from it, or dizziness, but rather a sensation of weight and pressure. These sensations, which were accompanied by various obsessing ideas, weighed very heavily on me and alarmed me'.

The rehearsals of *Mlada* brought a certain amount of distraction, but after a brilliantly successful *première* (October 20th/November 1st, 1892) the opera gradually fell into neglect, the public—including the Imperial family—preferring *Cavalleria Rusticana* and Tchaïkovsky's *Iolanta*. Among his friends, Rimsky-Korsakov himself made no secret of the fact that he considered the new work, elaborate as it was, 'far inferior to *Snow Maiden*'. His brain was playing him such tricks that on one occasion he could not remember the name of the latter opera. 'No, what-d'you-call-it', he said to his young friend and Eckermann,

Yastrebtsev, 'why, you know. . . . Not *Mlada*, no—the other one; I don't mean *May Night*. . . .' But his interest in music was not reawakened by either the production of *Mlada* or the exceptionally fine performances of *Snow Maiden* in Moscow in January, 1893, which drew him to the old capital —though the latter production left him with 'the conviction that *Snow Maiden* is not only my best opera but, on the whole, perhaps the best of all contemporary operas'. He simply went on with his study of philosophy until the renewal of the 'fatigue and unpleasant sensations in the head' became so serious that he was compelled to stop altogether. His doctor, diagnosing *Neurasthenia cerebrospinalis*, ordered complete mental rest and plenty of outdoor exercise. 'Not feeling the slightest inclination for manual work, I took long walks. . . . From time to time I read a little, but this brought on the old sensations and I was obliged, despondently, to leave off'. He handed over the conductorship of the Russian Symphony Concerts, which had begun to bore him the season before, to Glazunov and Lyadov, and he seldom appeared at Belaev's 'Fridays'. They, too, had 'fallen off in interest'. His brain was in such a curious state that the morning after the second concert of the season he asked Yastrebtsev why the latter had not attended the concert the night before, although Yastrebtsev had actually talked to him in the artists' room. The brief visit to Moscow in January brought welcome relief; for a week or two Rimsky-Korsakov even contemplated leaving indifferent Petersburg for the city 'where life seemed somehow younger and fresher'.

But he soon thought better of it. 'I must make an end of old-womanishness, illness and getting vexed with Balakirev, and get on with my work—that's all'.

Yet he was so disgusted not only with Balakirev's dictatorial methods, but the entire atmosphere of the Imperial Chapel, 'so saturated with spying, scandalmongering and toadyism', that he began to talk of resigning. Balakirev, being informed of his intention to leave 'for reasons of health', showed him every kindness and promised to see him liberally pensioned. But for one reason and another the resignation was postponed for nearly a year—till January, 1894.

Meanwhile little Masha's health grew steadily worse; she had already been ill for two and a half years. In the spring of 1893, her mother took her, with Nadya, to Yalta in the Crimea, hoping the climate of the Russian Riviera would save her. In May, as soon as the Conservatoire and Chapel examinations were over, their father hastened to join them, having been granted three months' leave from the Chapel. This summer at Yalta was the most wretched in Rimsky-Korsakov's life. He read, bathed and took long walks; but with his sick brain, and his little daughter dying under his eyes, all life had lost its savour. He tried to work at the orchestration and piano-score of *The Maid of Pskov*—he had hardly touched a piano for a whole year, he says—then turned restlessly to his writing and began some little textbooks 'which grew into philosophical treatises' and were afterwards burned. Finally he turned to the reminiscences begun years before, and spent much

of the sad, weary summer writing a great part of
that *Record of my Musical Life* with its sharp self-
criticism and its harsh judgments of old friends,
particularly of Balakirev. But he wrote it all
'dully and lifelessly'. 'I have never experienced
such lack of energy', he writes to his eldest son,
Misha, in these months of July and August. 'But
how can you be energetic when a weight is hang-
ing over you? . . . We have sunk into a sort of
mental torpor here; we live from day to day and
try not to speak of the future. . . . I can do
absolutely nothing in these days; the greater
part of the time I pace from one corner of the
room to another, or sit and smoke endlessly'. His
leave having expired, he left for Petersburg on
August 20th/September 1st, only to be over-
taken at Kharkov by a telegram announcing
Masha's death. The official quarters in the
Chapel buildings had now acquired so many
sad memories that, in view of his imminent
resignation, they moved at once to a new house.

CHAPTER VII

1893-96

Resigns from Imperial Chapel – desire to compose again –
Christmas Eve – *Sadko* as an opera – disillusionment with
Christmas Eve – 'I prefer to orchestrate rather than to compose'
– difficulties with the censorship – V. I. Belsky – addition to
Sadko – 'dreadful weariness' – Shalyapin's portrait of the composer – outraged Grand Dukes – 'revision' and reorchestration
of *Boris Godunov* – begins book on instrumentation.

CURIOUSLY enough, it was another death, that
of Tchaïkovsky in October, 1893, which rescued
Rimsky-Korsakov from his gloomy apathy. He
considered it a moral duty to dedicate the first
Russian Symphony Concert of the season to
Tchaïkovsky's memory; he was anxious to
conduct it [1]; and so, to Belaev's joy, he resumed
the direction of the series. Not only that but in
January, a week after his resignation from the
Imperial Chapel had taken effect, he·went with
Nadezhda to Odessa to conduct yet another
Tchaïkovsky memorial concert, and returned to
Petersburg feeling refreshed by the change.
Walking on the seashore at Odessa he had even
experienced a desire to compose again—on a
Homeric subject, the Nausicaa episode from the
Odyssey. But this plan was soon thrust aside by
another. And here, again, Tchaïkovsky's death
was a determining factor. Tchaïkovsky had
written an opera, *Vakula the Smith*, based on Gogol's
Christmas Eve, and although Rimsky-Korsakov had

[1] The following winter he had the less congenial duty of
opening the season with an Anton Rubinstein memorial concert.

long coveted the subject for himself he had feared
to hurt the other's feelings by appearing to enter
into rivalry with him. Now that obstacle was
removed and a private performance of his own
May Night, a sort of companion-piece, at his sister-
in-law's in April, decided him. He laid aside
Polonsky's libretto (written for Serov and used
by Tchaïkovsky), prepared one of his own, and
began to sketch out the music. Within a fortnight
he had not only written, but scored the introduction, and played it to his friends, asking them to
guess what it represented. For at first he made a
great mystery of his new opera, telling no one
what the subject was. 'Even if you guess right, I
shan't admit it', he told Yastrebtsev.

The summer of 1894 passed very differently
from that of the previous year. The Rimsky-
Korsakovs found a new country house at Vechasha
in the Luga district, with surroundings very like
those which had so happily inspired the composer
at Stelëvo. 'Vechasha is a charming spot', he
wrote, 'thanks to the wonderful great Lake Pesno
and a huge old garden with century-old elms and
lindens. . . . The bathing is lovely. At night the
moon and stars are marvellously reflected in the
lake. There are a host of birds'. In these surroundings *Christmas Eve* progressed rapidly. Not only
that but another long-meditated plan suddenly
ripened and thrust itself importunately on the
composer: an opera on the subject of *Sadko*.
Even as he worked at *Christmas Eve* the scenario of
Sadko began to take shape, with Stassov's assistance
by correspondence. Korsakov decided to draw
on the themes of his early orchestral piece as

leitmotives,[1] while other musical ideas began to
throng his head, 'for instance, the melody of
Sadko's aria, the theme of Nezhata's tale and part
of the finale of the opera. I remember that the
place where most of these ideas came to me was
the long bathing-stage built out into the lake
from the bank. It went out through the reeds;
on one side you saw the great slanting willows in
the garden, on the other spread Lake Pesno. All
this put me in the mood for *Sadko*. But the actual
composition of *Sadko* was laid aside till *Christmas
Eve* was finished'.

But if *Sadko* was, evidently, inspired and spontaneous, a good deal of *Christmas Eve* was manufactured—and the composer knew it. Even before
going to Vechasha he had talked of abandoning it
altogether. 'You know', he had said suddenly
to Yastrebtsev, after playing over part of the new
music, '*only lyrical music is good*, the rest is all *bad*.
It won't do for me to write the new opera—not
a bit. For there's nothing lyrical in me. And,
generally speaking, I'm no longer good for anything. If I ever had any creative power it's left
me—and for ever. And what a weak subject
this is, which I was so tremendously anxious to
compose only a little while ago!' And at
Vechasha, where Yastrebtsev visited them, there
was a similar scene one afternoon. Korsakov
began to play over what he had just composed but
suddenly broke off. '"No", he cried in a voice
full of sadness, even despair, "I can't play any

---

[1] Whereas in earlier days Rimsky-Korsakov had pronounced
the name of the piece with the stress on the first syllable, in the
Great Russian style, he now adopted the Ukrainian pronunciation
(and declension) with the stress on the second syllable.

more—it won't do. . . ." He began to walk
nervously up and down the room, looking at
nobody . . . he was obviously seriously agitated.
After dinner Korsakov had a short nap, while the
rest of us went into the field of rye to pick corn-
flowers for Nadya. When we came back, Nicholas
Andreevich, having mastered himself and his
nerves, played his new scene to the end. Nadezhda
Nikolaevna remained silent as before. Then
Korsakov got up, closed the music and this time,
not without humour, remarked: "Well, if my
future biographer wishes to describe the present
evening, he will be obliged to cry triumphantly:
The celebrated composer's second scene was
performed by the author himself amid the deathly
silence of the listeners!" This idea evidently
tickled him and he even began to cheer up!'
Nevertheless, he pressed on with the work and
before his return to Petersburg at the beginning of
September he had not only sketched out the whole
opera but orchestrated well over a hundred pages
of the score. 'How curious! I evidently prefer
to orchestrate rather than to compose', he writes
to Yastrebtsev.

The orchestration of *Christmas Eve* was finished
that winter, but in the meantime the libretto was
wrinkling brows in the censorship office owing to
the appearance in Scene Seven of a 'Tsaritsa',
anonymous, it is true, but obviously identifiable
through Gogol's story as Catherine the Great.
But fate was (temporarily) kind to Rimsky-
Korsakov. Balakirev having just resigned the
Directorship of the Imperial Chapel, the Court
Minister, Count Vorontsov-Dashkov, called on

Rimsky-Korsakov and offered him the vacant post. But the Chapel had become hateful; pensioned freedom was pleasant; and so he declined. Finding the Minister amiably disposed, however, Korsakov seized the opportunity to get him to arrange a special dispensation for the 'Empress' in *Christmas Eve*. Choral rehearsals began forthwith, and the composer was able to go back to Vechasha happily conscious of one new opera in course of production and another partly composed.

The greater part of *Sadko* was finished in reduced score during the summer of 1895. The work went easily and Korsakov never had to rest more than a day or two at a time. But in the middle of things he made an important addition to his plan. The previous winter he had met in St. Petersburg a shy, clever man, V. I. Belsky, lawyer, mathematician, amateur archæologist and warm admirer of Rimsky-Korsakov's music. Belsky spent the summer on an estate only five or six miles from Vechasha and was naturally a frequent visitor there. On his advice Korsakov (reverting to a suggestion made by Vladimir Stassov the year before) decided to introduce Sadko's wife into the action; this necessitated one entirely fresh scene, for which Belsky wrote the libretto, and additions to two other scenes. In the meantime the composer pressed on with the orchestration of the rest of the opera, working very hard till towards the end of the winter he was suddenly overpowered by 'dreadful weariness, loss of interest and almost dislike for work. This was the first time I had felt anything of the kind, but it reappeared afterwards towards the end of all my major works. It always came on suddenly; the composition would be going ahead splendidly, I would be keenly interested, and then all of a sudden I would be overcome by weariness and indifference. After a time this unpleasant mood would vanish and I would return to the work with all my former enthusiasm. This condition had nothing in common with that which had troubled me in 1891-93. I was troubled by no fearful fermentation of thoughts about philosophy and æsthetics'.

Christmas Eve was produced at the Maryinsky Theatre on November 21st/December 3rd, 1895, in a somewhat thunder - laden atmosphere. Shalyapin, then twenty-two and as yet unknown, who had only a minor part, has given us a graphic impression in his memoirs [1] of the composer as he saw him for the first time at the rehearsals: 'The magical composer impressed me by his extreme shyness and modesty. He was very unfashionably dressed; his black beard, that grew unchecked, flowed over a narrow, carelessly-knotted black stock, he wore a black frock-coat that was hopelessly out of date, and his trousér-pockets were inset horizontally in the manner of bygone days. He had two pairs of spectacles on his nose, one in front of the other. A deep crease between his brows gave him a melancholy look. He was profoundly silent. . . . At practically every rehearsal Napravnik, the conductor, would make some remark to the composer. For instance, he would say: "In my opinion, Nicholas Andreevich, this

[1] Published in English as *Man and Mask* (Victor Gollancz).

act drags—I suggest that you cut it". Rimsky-
Korsakov would get up, looking disturbed, lean
over the conductor's stand, and say in a somewhat tremulous and deprecatory voice: "Frankly,
I can't see that the act drags. . . ." Then,
hesitatingly, he would explain: "The construction of my work necessitates in this act a musical
interpretation of the theme which is the foundation
on which the rest of the opera rests". Where-
upon the cold, methodical voice of Napravnik
would reply, in a Czech accent and with pedantic
emphasis: "You may be right, but you are
influenced by love of your own work. You must
consider your public. . . . Years of experience
have convinced me that when a composer rigidly
refuses to alter a note of his music, the result is
often very long drawn out and wearisome to an
audience. I am saying all this because I really
feel for you. You'll have to condense it"'.

But everything had gone reasonably well up
to the *répétition générale*, which was unfortunately
attended by the Grand Dukes Vladimir Alexandrovich [1] and Michael Nikolaevich. The two
princes were outraged almost beyond words at
finding their illustrious ancestress portrayed upon
the stage. The Grand Duke Michael particularly
objected to the Petropavlovsk Fortress being
painted as part of the scenery, on the ground that
his ancestors were buried in it, while the Grand

[1] The Grand Duke Vladimir Alexandrovich almost deserves a
chapter to himself in the history of Russian music. He afterwards became Dyagilev's patron, but the refinement of his
musical taste may be judged by his request to Tchaïkovsky that
the poor composer would arrange the 'Dance of the Blue Bird'
from *The Sleeping Beauty* for two cornets with military band
accompaniment.

Duke Vladimir's finer feelings were so pained by
the outrage on the Empress Catherine that at the
interval he hastened behind the scenes and,
sarcastically addressing the singer who had taken
the part, said, 'You are now my great-grand-
mother, I perceive'. 'Which', says the composer,
'upset her not a little'. The Tsar forthwith withdrew his permission for the production in that
form and Vsevolozhsky, the Director, in despair,
saved the situation by 'translating' the mezzo-
soprano 'Tsaritsa' (like Bottom) into a baritone
'Serene Highness', thereby reducing the central
incident of the plot to absurdity and, if he had
but seen it, making the Imperial family appear
more ridiculous still. The Tsar was mollified
but the Imperial family showed their displeasure
by staying away from the *première*, and the composer demonstrated *his* disapproval of the outrage
on Gogol and himself by staying away too. But
his children went, and the faithful Yastrebtsev
brought home a wreath for him.

It is amusing to observe that the very month
after this mutilation of his own work, Rimsky-
Korsakov began that 'revision' and reorchestration of Mussorgsky's *Boris* which has brought such
wrath on his well-meaning, pedantic head. The
impertinence of 'correcting' and 'improving' his
dead friend's completed work seemed to him, of
course, merely a pendant to his earlier task of
completing and issuing Mussorgsky's unfinished
works; it was carried out in the same spirit.
There is delightful irony in these 'improvements'
being made by one who was so quick to resent
Balakirev's corrections of *his* work, these slashing

cuts by a composer whose supreme grievance was that almost every one of his own operas had been cut by Napravnik.

This 'repainting' of *Boris* having been completed in May, 1896, Rimsky-Korsakov returned to *Sadko*, taking it with him to a new summer residence at Shmerdovitsï and finishing it in September. Nadya and Volodya were down with the measles, but otherwise he had no troubles but his own fits of fatigue, of which he relates a curious instance (hardly confirmed, however, by the dates on the autograph score). Having just completed the last scene but one, Korsakov says he was overcome by one of these 'fits of disgust' at having yet another to do. It was only in turning over his pile of manuscript that he discovered the score of this last scene already completed. Yet he found time that summer also to make notes for another book on instrumentation. And this time they were not destroyed.

CHAPTER VIII

1896–1904

Outburst of song-writing – 'genuine vocal music'' – *Mozart and Salieri* – *Switezianka* – great industry – the Mamontov opera company – *Boyarinya Vera Sheloga* – *The Tsar's Bride* – Korsakov's operas performed outside Russia – various opera plans – *Tsar Saltan* – *The Song of Oleg the Wise* – new figures in the Belaev circle – *Servilia* – escape from nationalism – new spirit in the Imperial Theatres – thirty-fifth anniversary celebrations – *Pan Voevoda* – the 'prelude-cantata' *From Homer* – *Kashchey the Immortal* – *The Stone Guest* re-scored and revised – meets the young Stravinsky – *Kitezh* – 'art is the most enchanting of lies' – death of M. P. Belaev – *On the Tomb*.

WITH *Sadko* Rimsky-Korsakov reached the highest peak of his creative activity since *Snow Maiden*. It is, as he was fully conscious, one of his finest works, the consummation of an epic-fantastic operatic genre, peculiarly his own. Perhaps it was this feeling that *Sadko* was unsurpassable in its kind which sent him during the next few years on a curious career of operatic exploration, beginning the year after *Sadko* with a complete reversion to Dargomïzhskian 'dramatic truth' in his setting of Pushkin's 'little tragedy' *Mozart and Salieri*. But the immediate sequel to *Sadko* was a tremendous spate of songs (with a few vocal duets), the opus-numbers running from 39 to 56 almost without a break. 'I had written no songs for a long time', he says. 'Turning to Alexey Tolstoy's poems, I set four of them'—Op. 39—'and felt that I was now composing in a different way. The melodies, following the text, turned out purely vocally, with no more than hints of

harmony and modulation. I worked out the
accompaniments after the melodies were finished,
whereas before, with few exceptions, the melodies
had been conceived more or less instrumentally—
i.e. agreeing only with the general feeling of the
text, even derived from the harmonic basis of the
song'.

Feeling that his new way of composing had
produced 'genuine vocal music', he embarked on
it with reckless industry. By the spring of 1897
he had not only begun to sketch *Mozart and Salieri*
and made yet another revision and reorchestration
of *Antar*, but had written a score of songs. As for
the summer, a letter to Kruglikov, written at the
end of September after his return from the
country, speaks for itself: 'The news that I've
composed thirty-nine songs and the opera *Mozart
and Salieri* is really false, for I've written forty
songs, two duets, *Mozart and Salieri*, a cantata
Switezianka for soprano, tenor, chorus and orchestra,
and besides that a trio for piano, violin and 'cello,
but only in sketches, which will now be worked
up; all the rest, i.e. *Mozart and Salieri* and *Switezianka* are completely scored. Having returned
to Petersburg in September, I wrote something
else—will tell you about it later. Perhaps you're
surprised. But there's nothing surprising in all
this; it's how things ought to be. Thirty years
have passed since the days when Stassov used to
write that in 186–, such-and-such-a-year, the
Russian School had been extremely active:
Lodïzhensky had written one song, Borodin was
planning something, Balakirev intended to alter
something else, etc. It's time I left that sort of

thing behind and took a normal artistic path'. [1]
(Nor does he add that he had also written a
number of fugal exercises that summer.) The
'something else' was a String Quartet in G which,
like the trio, remained unpublished, 'since both
these productions convinced me that chamber
music is not my sphere'. Instead he resumed his
book on orchestration.

In the autumn *Sadko* was submitted to the
Theatre Directorate. But after *Christmas Eve*
Rimsky-Korsakov was regarded as a scapegrace.
The trial run-through at the piano turned out
badly and was broken off 'owing to the lateness
of the hour'. Without definitely refusing the
work, Vsevolozhsky hummed and hawed and
Rimsky-Korsakov decided in a huff that he
'would never trouble the Directorate with his
operas again'. As a matter of fact he was already
secure in the knowledge that another means of
production was open to him. Even in the summer
S. I. Mamontov, the railway magnate, who ran an
excellent opera company of his own in Moscow,
had been inquiring about *Sadko*. Now Korsakov
sent him the score, and the first performance of
the opera was accordingly given under Esposito
in the Solodovnikovsky Theatre in Moscow on

[1] Compare this with Tchaïkovsky's remark in a letter to
Nadezhda von Meck: 'One must always *work*, and a self-
respecting artist must not fold his hands on the pretext that he
isn't in the mood. If one waited for the *mood* without going
half-way to meet it, one would very easily become *lazy* and
apathetic. . . . I have learned to master myself and am glad
I've not followed in the footsteps of those of my Russian colleagues
who have no self-confidence and no patience, and who throw
up the sponge at the slightest difficulty. That is why, in spite
of their great gifts, they produce so little and in such a desultory
way'.

December 26th (January 7th, 1898). It was a bad, under-rehearsed performance, but a few weeks later the Mamontov company visited Petersburg and opened its season in the Conservatoire Theatre with a very fine production of *Sadko*, conducted by the composer himself.

Rimsky-Korsakov's industry at this period was so unflagging that the story of his life becomes little more than a record of work done. In the spring of 1898 he reconstructed the Prologue to *The Maid of Pskov* (omitted from the final version) as a separate one-act opera *Boyarinya Vera Sheloga*, and began a full-length opera on a long-cherished subject, Mey's melodramatic play, *The Tsar's Bride*. In accordance with the general trend of his ideas he was determined to make the work 'above all, singable'. And he wrote the part of the heroine specially for the voice of Nadezhda Zabela, one of the ladies of Mamontov's company, who had sung the part of the Sea Princess in *Sadko* and who, perhaps, aroused in him something more than a purely artistic interest. At any rate he corresponded with her frequently, though only fragments from the letters have as yet been published. Zabela's voice certainly inspired one extraordinarily lovely song, and there are other fine pages in *The Tsar's Bride*, but the work—more than a little suggestive of Bizet-with-a-Russian accent—is a mournful decline from *Sadko*. The actual composition and the orchestration of nearly two acts were done very quickly during the summer (again spent at Vechasha, which they had deserted for the last two years). The score was finished in November and produced by the

Mamontov company in October, 1899. In the
meantime Mamontov in the last months of 1898
brought out *Mozart and Salieri, Vera Sheloga*, and the
new version of *The Maid* (Shalyapin scoring a tremendous success as Ivan the Terrible) in Moscow,
repeating them in Petersburg in the new year,
while officialdom in the person of Vsevolozhsky
made a gesture of reconciliation by reviving *Snow
Maiden*[1] with new costumes and scenery—magnificent but all wrong, in the composer's view. 'Father
Frost', for instance, 'looked more like Father
Neptune'. Korsakov's operas also began to cross
the frontier. Prague accepted them warmly, but
May Night suffered a fiasco at Frankfurt-am-Main
in May, 1900.

Nor was Rimsky-Korsakov in the mood to rest
on his laurels. With Belsky he discussed various
possible opera subjects during that winter of
1898–99: Pushkin's *Legend of Tsar Saltan*, a work
in which the legend of the Invisible City of Kitezh
could be linked with that of St. Fevronia of
Murom, Byron's *Heaven and Earth, Odysseus at the
Court of Alkinous*. But the choice fell on *Tsar
Saltan*; Belsky himself undertook to prepare a
libretto from Pushkin's text; and the summer at
Vechasha again brought forth a nearly complete
opera, one infinitely more delightful and characteristic than its predecessor. Also from the
summer of 1899 dates a piece of 'relaxation',
as the composer called it, a cantata, *The Song of
Oleg the Wise*. The score of *Saltan* was completed
on January 19th/31st, 1900, but owing to a

In the orchestration of which the composer had made
changes substantial enough to justify the issue of a revised score.

passing unpleasantness with Belaev these new works, including the concert suite of 'musical pictures' from *Tsar Saltan*, were published by Bessel. New figures were appearing in the Belaev circle, not only Rimsky-Korsakov's own young men, but less congenial strangers from Moscow—notably Skryabin. 'Signs of decadence from the West began to appear'. The ardent young modernist of the sixties, the leader and teacher of the eighties, was in danger of surviving in the new century only as a back-number. Certainly the work which he began immediately after *Saltan* must have confirmed any detached observer in that view.

Rimsky-Korsakov's lifelong attachment to such a fourth-rate dramatist as Mey is incomprehensible, for in each case, except *The Maid of Pskov*, Mey inspired his weakest operas. 'Oh, how I want to write an opera!' the composer wrote to Zabela in April, 1900. But he wanted it above all things to be non-Russian; he wanted 'freedom of style', escape from the nationalism he had practised so successfully and which had so long seemed to him the very mainspring of artistic creation. Accordingly, he took the Way of the Cross, finding in Mey's *Servilia*, a melodrama of ancient Rome complete with senators, centurions and persecuted Christian maidens, the necessary pretext for writing colourless music. It must be admitted that he took the fullest advantage of it. Returning from a brief visit to Brussels in March—he had refused more than one such invitation to Paris—he began *Servilia* at once. But it was finished abroad. Andrey Rimsky-Korsakov was studying his own country; in December, 1900, the thirty-fifth anniversary of his first public appearance as a composer was celebrated by special concerts organized by various societies (though *not* by the Imperial Theatres), dinners, addresses and presentations. 'I was very grateful for all this but it was intolerably boring and upsetting. . . . Really, to hear every day: "Deeply respected Nicholas Andreevich, during thirty-five years . . ." or "Thirty-five years have now passed since . . .", etc. is intolerable. And what is more I don't believe in the perfect sincerity of all this. I can't help feeling that my jubilee was used in some cases as a pretext for other people to advertise and draw attention to themselves'.

Rimsky-Korsakov was at this time wavering, between no fewer than four opera subjects. With Belsky he constantly discussed *Kitezh* and *Nausicaa*, and Belsky even began the libretto of the latter. But the composer also wanted to write a Polish opera, partly as a tribute to Chopin, whom he had long worshipped, partly because he wanted to introduce in it some melodies his mother had heard in the days when his father had held a Polish governorship and which she had sung to him as a baby. He commissioned a librettist to prepare an original 'book', *Pan Voevoda*, on lines laid down by himself: plenty of drama, no politics, a slight fantastic element and plenty of dancing. The libretto was written and, poor as it was, he seems to have liked it. At the same time someone else offered him the libretto of a short fantastic opera on a subject from Russian folk-lore, *Kashchey the Immortal*. He liked the subject but was not

entirely satisfied with the libretto. It was ᴀ
curious dilemma. But having put the finishing
touches to the orchestration of *Servilia* in May,
1901, he began a sort of prelude-cantata for
female voices and orchestra which was to form
the introduction to *Nausicaa*. However, he soon
laid it aside and took up the *Kashchey* libretto
which, with the help of his daughter Sonya, he
altered to his liking. He determined to issue his
'prelude-cantata' as an independent work, *From
Homer*, Op. 60, and in the meantime went ahead
with the surprisingly modern (if not particularly
Russian) music of *Kashchey*, finishing the first two
scenes by the beginning of September. Having
completed and scored the whole work in the
course of the winter, Rimsky-Korsakov turned
industriously to *Pan Voevoda* and not only completed that very dull work during the summer and
autumn of 1902 (all but the orchestration), but
actually re-scored Dargomïzhsky's *Stone Guest*
during the same period. He had long been
dissatisfied with his own youthful orchestration;
no one blames him for that, of course. But he
characteristically took the opportunity to 'soften
some of the extreme harshness and the harmonic
crudities of the original', a labour rather less
praiseworthy.

The bulk of this work, *Pan Voevoda* and the new
edition of *The Stone Guest*, was done during July
and August at Heidelberg, where Andrey was
now studying and where he introduced to his
father a fellow-student named Igor Stravinsky.
They again spent the vacation in Switzerland
and returned leisurely by way of Munich, Dresden

his own country; in Decem[ber]
fifth anniversary of his first [appearance] the thirty-
as a composer was celebrated by appearance
organized by various societies (th[e] concerts
the Imperial Theatres), dinners, ad[...]not by
presentations. 'I was very grateful for and
but it was intolerably boring and upsetting this
Really, to hear every day: "Deeply respec[t]
Nicholas Andreevich, during thirty-five years . . .
or "Thirty-five years have now passed since . . .",
etc. is intolerable. And what is more I don't
believe in the perfect sincerity of all this. I can't
help feeling that my jubilee was used in some cases
as a pretext for other people to advertise and draw
attention to themselves'.

Rimsky-Korsakov was at this time wavering
between no fewer than four opera subjects. With
Belsky he constantly discussed *Kitezh* and *Nausicaa*,
and Belsky even began the libretto of the latter.
But the composer also wanted to write a Polish
opera, partly as a tribute to Chopin, whom he
had long worshipped, partly because he wanted
to introduce in it some melodies his mother had
heard in the days when his father had held a
Polish governorship and which she had sung to
him as a baby. He commissioned a librettist to
prepare an original 'book', *Pan Voevoda*, on lines
laid down by himself: plenty of drama, no politics,
a slight fantastic element and plenty of dancing.
The libretto was written and, poor as it was, he
seems to have liked it. At the same time someone
else offered him the libretto of a short fantastic
opera on a subject from Russian folk-lore, *Kashchey
the Immortal*. He liked the subject but was not

d with the libretto. It was ι
entirely ima. But having put the finishing
curio the orchestration of *Servilia* in May,
touc began a sort of prelude-cantata for
190 voices and orchestra which was to form
ᶠᵉ introduction to *Nausicaa*. However, he soon
it aside and took up the *Kashchey* libretto
which, with the help of his daughter Sonya, he
altered to his liking. He determined to issue his
'prelude-cantata' as an independent work, *From
Homer*, Op. 60, and in the meantime went ahead
with the surprisingly modern (if not particularly
Russian) music of *Kashchey*, finishing the first two
scenes by the beginning of September. Having
completed and scored the whole work in the
course of the winter, Rimsky-Korsakov turned
industriously to *Pan Voevoda* and not only completed that very dull work during the summer and
autumn of 1902 (all but the orchestration), but
actually re-scored Dargomïzhsky's *Stone Guest*
during the same period. He had long been
dissatisfied with his own youthful orchestration;
no one blames him for that, of course. But he
characteristically took the opportunity to 'soften
some of the extreme harshness and the harmonic
crudities of the original', a labour rather less
praiseworthy.

The bulk of this work, *Pan Voevoda* and the new
edition of *The Stone Guest*, was done during July
and August at Heidelberg, where Andrey was
now studying and where he introduced to his
father a fellow-student named Igor Stravinsky.
They again spent the vacation in Switzerland
and returned leisurely by way of Munich, Dresden

and Berlin in time to hear the *première* of *Servilia*
under Felix Blumenfeld at the Maryinsky Theatre
on October 1st/14th, while *Kashchey* was brought
out in Moscow by the ex-Mamontov company
just two months later (December 12th/25th).

Even before the scoring of the Polish opera was
finished, in the spring of 1903, Rimsky-Korsakov
began the sketches of *Kitezh*. The bulk of the
composition was roughed out by the autumn, the
rest, with most of the scoring, being completed
during the summer of 1904 at Vechasha. The
Christian ideology of *Kitezh* not unnaturally
suggests that Rimsky-Korsakov had abandoned
his lifelong rationalism for a faith definitely
Christian, if by no means Orthodox, particularly
when we find in it such a strong element of that
imaginative pantheism with which his rationalism
had always been so strongly tempered. It is
possible, but improbable. In considering the
relation between Korsakov's life and his work it
is of the highest importance to recall a saying
recorded by Yastrebtsev, even though the saying
dates from December, 1893, the period of crisis
and depression: 'I doubt if you would find anyone
in the whole world more incredulous of everything
supernatural, fantastic, phantasmal or lying
beyond the grave, and yet as an artist it is just
these things that I love above all. And *ceremonial*—
what could be more intolerable than ceremonial?
. . . Yet with what delight I have depicted
"ceremonial" in music! No—I'm definitely of
the opinion that art is essentially the most enchanting and intoxicating of lies!' That view would,
of course, explain the fundamental weakness of so

H

much of his music. On the other hand, in May, 1907, a little more than a year before his death, he wrote to Glazunov that 'generally speaking "there is no truth on earth"—although that is itself untrue, for truth does exist on earth, but only in science and art'.

In the last days of December, 1903, M. P. Belaev died, leaving a triumvirate of Rimsky-Korsakov, Glazunov and Lyadov to administer the vast fortune he had bequeathed to Russian music: the continuance of the publishing house, the Russian Symphony Concerts, the Glinka Prizes for orchestral works, the chamber music competition schemes, and the fund for the assistance of needy musicians. Rimsky-Korsakov at once wrote a memorial piece, a short orchestral prelude, *On the Tomb*, which opened the first Russian Symphony Concert of the season (February 19th/March 3rd), conducting it himself. But for the most part he now left the conducting of these concerts to the younger men.

CHAPTER IX

1904–1908

SUMMER—the summer that Chekhov died in Germany, while thousands of Russians were dying round Port Arthur—passed peacefully with the work of *Kitezh* and more plans for the book on orchestration. The disasters of the Japanese War wounded Rimsky-Korsakov's patriotic pride, but he could have had no suspicion that the repercussions of the war were to affect his own fate. But when in November the Imperial Theatres at last produced his version of *Boris*, with Shalyapin as the hero, the authorities soon thought it advisable to cut out the insurrection scene 'near Kromy'. Everywhere in Russia the revolutionary elements had been encouraged by the reverses of the war; in January, 1905, Petersburg was practically in a state of revolution. The student class as usual were foremost in the disturbances, those of the Conservatoire among the rest. They held illegal meetings and the 'cowardly and tactless' Director, Rimsky-Korsakov's former pupil Bernhard (backed by the heads of the Russian Music Society, the body which had founded the Conservatoire and still exercised a certain control over it), began to devise repressive measures: the expulsion of the ringleaders, the bringing of police into the building, even the closing of the Conservatoire. Rimsky-Korsakov stood up for the rights of the students and was in consequence regarded by the conservative members of the staff 'almost as the leader of the revolutionary movement among the students'. Bernhard continued to 'behave tactlessly' and Korsakov brought things to a head by publishing in the paper *Russ* (in amplification of a briefly reported speech) a letter advocating the emancipation of the Conservatoire from the control of the R.M.S. Bernhard took exception to the letter at a sitting of the Council of the Conservatoire; words ran high; and Bernhard cut short the meeting. On March 16th/29th, the Conservatoire building being surrounded by mounted and foot police, Rimsky-Korsakov with a number of the other professors sent the Director a written demand for his resignation and within three days the higher authorities settled the matter 'impartially' by the dismissal of both Bernhard and Rimsky-Korsakov, the expulsion of more than a hundred students, and the temporary closing of the Conservatoire. Rimsky-Korsakov, having retorted by sending another letter to the Press and by resigning his honorary membership of the Russian Music

Society, at once found himself the martyr-hero of liberal and intellectual Russia. From every part of the country came a flood of letters and addresses of sympathy both from institutions and individuals. Deputations from various societies visited him and the Press was full of the affair. The Directorate were abused high and low and some of its members resigned, while Glazunov, Lyadov, Felix Blumenfeld and one or two other members of the Conservatoire staff also resigned in sympathy with Rimsky-Korsakov. Rimsky-Korsakov and Glazunov each orchestrated one of the popular revolutionary songs of the day: Korsakov 'Dubinushka'; Glazunov, the all too celebrated 'Volga Boat Song'.

Matters reached a climax on March 27th/April 9th, when the students gave a concert, conducted by Glazunov, in the Komissarzhevsky Theatre. The first part was to consist of *Kashchey*, the second of a miscellaneous programme. But after *Kashchey* the affair became a political demonstration, almost a revolutionary meeting. 'They called me on the platform and began to read me addresses from different societies and associations and to make inflammatory speeches. They say that some-body yelled "Down with the autocracy!" The uproar after each address and speech was in-describable', Rimsky-Korsakov tells us. Finally the police intervened, lowered the iron safety-curtain, and cleared the hall. Fearing a repeti-tion of this demonstration the Petersburg police suppressed the next Russian Symphony Concert, announced for four days later, and forbade the performance of any of Rimsky-Korsakov's com-

positions. Their example was followed in certain
provincial centres, with the natural result that
when the ban was lifted after a couple of months
or so his music enjoyed far more popularity than
ever before.

All this might have intoxicated a man of more
flamboyant temperament, but Rimsky-Korsakov,
shy and scholarly if obstinate and a little hot-
tempered when roused, longed for peace. He
withdrew to Vechasha, badly ruffled, depressed
and in no 'mood for composition, resumed the
Record of my Musical Life after a break of twelve
years (though again, as it happened, in a melancholy mood), and began a very interesting
thematic analysis of his *Snow Maiden*. Writing
at the beginning of July to Nadezhda, who had
gone to Bad Nauheim with Andrey, he said:
'I feel it's time I began to occupy myself with
musico-literary work instead of composition;
I'm very much afraid of doing something weak
and letting myself down. In any case, after ten
years of intense creative activity it will be a good
thing to stop or wait a bit. In former years I used
to allow myself a break here, but I haven't done
so for ten years. Besides, music is now beginning
to enter on a sort of new and incomprehensible
phase of development (Strauss, d'Indy, Debussy,
etc.). But I and many of us—well, we belong to
a different, earlier period'. After a week or so
he broke off his analysis of *Snow Maiden* and
began to work more steadily at his book on the
orchestra, continuing this after his return to
Petersburg.

The Conservatoire remained closed, though

pupils came privately to Rimsky - Korsakov's
house, and the political air was still thunder-laden.
The production of *Pan Voevoda* in Moscow in
September, under Rakhmaninov, could not be
advertised owing to a strike of printers. In
October there was an all-Russian general strike,
suppressed only with bloodshed. The R.M.S.
was sadly discredited in consequence of the events
of the beginning of the year, and even the Russian
Symphony Concerts were in financial difficulty.
All Rimsky-Korsakov's public actions savoured of
defiance; his *Dubinushka* was played at a Ziloti concert in November and a little later he organized
a concert in aid of the families of destitute workers.
The Director of the Imperial Theatres was obliged
to *ask permission* to produce *Kitezh*, since the
composer flatly refused to submit it in the usual
way. Even the reopening of the Conservatoire,
with a fresh and slightly freer constitution, brought
more unpleasantness. Rimsky-Korsakov and the
professors who had resigned or been dismissed
were invited to return, the expelled pupils were
allowed to come back, and the Council of Professors was requested to elect a new Director.
But although Glazunov was unanimously chosen,
he soon came into conflict with the conservative
members of the Council. There were more
stormy scenes and on January 26th/February 8th,
1906, Korsakov lost his temper and walked out,
saying that he would have nothing more to do
with the Conservatoire; he was fetched back and
pacified; but it was some time before he could
be persuaded to give up the idea of resignation.
His nerves were far too upset to compose, though

he brooded over various subjects—a 'mystery' based on Byron's *Heaven and Earth*, for which he made notes once more, and an opera on *Stenka Razin*. Instead, he turned again to Mussorgsky's works, restoring the cuts he had made in *Boris* —though not the original harmonies and so on— and having persuaded Stassov (who died a few months later) to let him have the score of the uncompleted opera *Marriage*, for publication, began to orchestrate it.

In June with his son and daughter, Volodya and Nadya, he travelled south by way of Vienna to Riva on Lake Garda, where they were joined by his wife and Andrey and where he orchestrated a few songs, his own and Mussorgsky's, and touched up *Dubinushka* and *Kashchey*. And, after an expedition through the North Italian cities— Milan, Genoa, Florence and Venice—he completed at Riva the *Record of my Musical Life*, dating it 'August 22nd, old style', the eve of their return to Russia. 'It is rather muddled, not equally detailed throughout, and written in a bad literary style, often very drily; but there is *nothing in it but the truth*. . . .' (Which is unfortunately *not* quite true, for it contains numerous unintentional inaccuracies.) And the last paragraphs are overcast with autumnal melancholy. 'The thought that it is time to end my career as a composer, which has pursued me ever since I finished *Kitezh*, has not left me here. . . . I don't want to find myself in the ridiculous position of "a singer who has lost his voice". We shall see what time will bring. . . .' He had not long to wait. Within six weeks of his return to Petersburg his notebooks contained the cockcrow theme of *The Golden Cockerel.*

Belsky had undertaken the construction of a libretto from Pushkin's fairy-tale satire on stupid autocracy. By the middle of November the new work was well under way and Yastrebtsev was able to note in his diary that 'N.A. is obviously awfully glad to be composing again'. Before the end of the year the First Act was finished as far as the entrance of the Astrologer, the full score being made first this time and the piano reduction afterwards. At about the same time Rimsky-Korsakov acquired a fresh private pupil, Igor Stravinsky, who with his brother Gury had for some time been a member of the circle which attended the Rimsky-Korsakovs' Wednesday evening music-makings. By a curious chance the appearance of this new pupil exactly coincided with the celebration of the twenty-fifth anniversary of the début of an old one, Glazunov. Korsakov naturally took a leading part in the commemorations.

Rehearsals of *Kitezh*, one of the finest of all Rimsky-Korsakov's works, had been going on at the Maryinsky Theatre throughout the winter, and Felix Blumenfeld conducted the first performance on February 7th/20, 1907. The ovations began at the end of the First Act and the triumph was complete. 'The *Cockerel* doesn't get on very well, what with all these concerts and jubilees and rehearsals', the composer complained to Yastrebtsev. And Dyagilev was urging him to go to Paris in May for the festival of five Russian orchestral concerts he had organized. For a

while Rimsky-Korsakov held out, then consented
in the words of a humorous catch-phrase: 'Here
goes—as the parrot said when the cat hauled him
out of the cage'. Ten days before he set out—
with his wife, Nadya, Andrey and Volodya—
Maximilian Steinberg had played through the
manuscript First Act of the *Cockerel* to a small
audience which included Belsky, Yastrebtsev and
Igor Stravinsky. This Act was already orchestrated and the Second well under way.

Dyagilev's Paris programmes included the
orchestral suites from *Christmas Eve* and *Tsar
Saltan* and excerpts from *Mlada*, *Sadko* and *Snow
Maiden*. Korsakov himself conducted two or
three numbers, Nikisch the others. He did not
wish to direct a whole programme and declined
all invitations to conduct after his return to
Russia. During this visit to Paris he had one
more brush with the 'new and incomprehensible'
music and its composers, not only the *Poem of
Ecstasy* of Skryabin, who was in Paris with a host
of other Russian composers and whom Korsakov
had always disliked (the man as much as his
music), but Strauss and Debussy. He heard
Strauss conduct *Salome* at the Châtelet and was
introduced to Strauss by Colonne. Glazunov
has told us that Rimsky-Korsakov heard *Pelléas et
Mélisande* at the Opéra-Comique and said, 'I will
have nothing more to do with this music, lest I
should unhappily develop a liking for it'. With
two members of the Imperial family who happened
to be in Paris Rimsky-Korsakov would have no
contact; in spite of kind invitations, he would
neither attend the Grand Duke Paul Alex-

androvich's party nor join the Grand Duchess
Maria Pavlovna in her box at the Opéra. He was
much more interested in getting *Sadko* produced
at the Grand Opéra and when Dyagilev's lieutenant, Calvocoressi, pointed out that without cuts
(to which the composer would agree only as a
last resource) it was very long, he replied with the
amazing suggestion: 'If it is found too long for
one evening, why not give it in two halves?'

Returning to Russia in June, Rimsky-Korsakov
settled for the summer on the beautiful estate of
Lyubensk, which he thought of buying—it was
quite near Vechasha, on high ground overlooking
his beloved Lake Pesno—and there resumed work
on *The Golden Cockerel*, completing the full score
of Act II and the sketches of Act III by the end of
August. Glazunov wrote to him from Folkestone
sounding him as to his willingness to accept an
honorary doctorate from Oxford or Cambridge,
adding his personal assurance that 'the ceremony
is by no means tiring and there's no need to make
a speech'. But Korsakov replied (June 20th/
July 3rd): 'I most decidedly don't want to be
made a doctor of Oxford or Cambridge University: first, because I don't consider such honorary
degrees appropriate to composers in general and
to myself in particular (perhaps that's only a
whim of mine, but there it is); secondly, because
I don't intend to go to England. Of course, you
must only mention the second reason . . . and
give my thanks to those who commissioned you
to approach me for the—in their opinion—
flattering and complimentary intention'. But in
November, whether he liked it or not, he was

elected a corresponding member of the 'Académie des Beaux Arts', in the place of Grieg who had just died. The political alliance between France and Russia was arousing in France an ever keener interest in Russian art, and (conversely) important people in Russia were backing Dyagilev with the idea of fostering sympathy between the two countries—of all of which Rimsky-Korsakov was quite aware and slightly. contemptuous. Nevertheless, while Dyagilev was meditating the production of *Sadko* at the Grand Opéra, Albert Carré was also actively preparing *Snow Maiden* at the Opéra-Comique and N. N. Cherepnin went to Paris to supervise it for the composer. It is fortunate that Korsakov could not foresee the fell use to which Dyagilev was to put *Sheherazade*, for in January, 1908, he wrote of Isadora Duncan: 'I haven't seen her once. I dare say she is very graceful, a beautiful mime, and so on; but what I dislike about her is that she connects her art with musical compositions dear to me. . . . How vexed I should be if I learned that Miss Duncan danced and mimed to my *Sheherazade*, *Antar* or *Easter Overture*.

On February 16th/29th, 1908, the day after the first Moscow performance of *Kitezh*, Felix Blumenfeld conducted the 'Introduction and Wedding Procession' from *The Golden Cockerel* at a Russian Symphony Concert. Nine days later the dramatic censor refused to sanction the libretto without cuts: forty-five lines in all. 'So the *Cockerel* won't come out in Russia', Rimsky-Korsakov wrote defiantly to the publisher Jurgenson. 'For I don't intend to change any·

thing. Perhaps it will do in Paris'. A French translation had already been prepared. 'Both Belsky and I are very pleased with it', he wrote. 'Calvocoressi has got on the right track'. But a day or two later he seemed more willing to compromise. Belsky and Telyakovsky, the Director of the Theatres, who was a genuine artist and an admirer of Korsakov's work,[1] soon induced him to agree to a few alterations. Jurgenson, who was going ahead with the printing, received a letter asking his 'much respected proof-reader not to smother the sheets with question-marks; where there are obvious mistakes let him correct them. I'm not a Richard Strauss and I don't write false harmonies on purpose. . . .' Rimsky-Korsakov, it may be mentioned, always gave the proofs of his full scores to pupils whom he knew could not afford to pay one hundred and fifty rubles for a score.

Already on his birthday Rimsky-Korsakov had complained of his heart, difficulty of breathing and so on; and on April 10th/23rd, after sitting up late into the night, discussing his book on instrumentation with Steinberg (who was now betrothed to Nadya), he had a severe attack of *angina pectoris*. Accustomed to activity, he could not be induced to rest and a second attack followed five days later. He had to be given oxygen and morphia, and the doctor ordered complete rest, the giving-up of smoking, a strict diet—no coffee

[1] The 'diminutive ex-colonel of Horse Guards' described in Theodore Komissarzhevsky's *Myself and the Theatre*. He managed the Imperial Theatres brilliantly from 1901 till the Revolution and 'died in misery a few years later, forgotten by nearly everyone'.

or meat—and no visitors. For a week the
composer stayed obediently in his bedroom, then,
assisted - by Steinberg, began to occupy himself
with the proofs of the *Cockerel* and work at his
book on the orchestra. He was allowed one
visitor a day. Glazunov was the first, and then
came Lyadov, Cui, Belsky, Yastrebtsev and
others. From Paris came telegrams announcing
the success of the interpolations he had made in
Boris at Dyagilev's request and of *Snow Maiden* at
the Opéra-Comique. He seemed much better
and went to Lyubensk on May 21st/June 3rd.
Two days before, he had gathered from a tele-
phone conversation with Telyakovsky that the
Cockerel might be given in Petersburg that season,
but not in Moscow. Still, Zimin's private company were willing to give it at once in Moscow.
But a few days later came a blow. `The Governor
of Moscow had forbidden the production there
and Telyakovsky had fears of a similar veto in
Petersburg. The authorities were willing enough
to use Korsakov to dress their political shop-
window in Paris. But the satirical *Cockerel* at
home—that was a different matter.

The first night at Lyubensk Rimsky-Korsakov
had a fresh attack from which he quickly recovered.
He worked at his book and was able to walk
'slowly and not very much' in his garden, delighting in the lilacs, the acacias and the apple-trees
in bloom. On Wednesday, June 4th/17th, Nadya
was married quite simply in the village church to
Maximilian Steinberg, but her father was not
present at the ceremony and the next day he had
a particularly bad attack. On the Friday he

wrote to Jurgenson expressing his indignation at Telyakovsky's news and at .Telyakovsky's 'being frightened by the Moscow scarecrow'; on the Saturday he wrote a few more pages of his book. In the early hours of Sunday the 8th/21st, after a short but severe thunderstorm, he had another attack and died.

Two days later, after a service in the chapel of the St. Petersburg Conservatoire, he was buried in the cemetery of the Novodevichy Monastery in St. Petersburg.

.   .   .   .   .   .

Looking back on Rimsky-Korsakov's work as a whole, one sees at once that the Korsakov who matters is Korsakov the opera-composer. True, his first three operas were squeezed out at rather long intervals and he was forty-five before he definitely devoted himself to the stage. But, broadly speaking, his non-operatic music, other than the charming early orchestral works and the later trio of masterpieces, is negligible. Even the best of his concert-works for orchestra are hardly 'symphonic' in the true sense; their delightful material and magical scoring have deservedly won them a unique place in the repertoire, but they reveal the composer's lack of skill as a musical architect all too clearly. In the field of opera, however, lack of symphonic mastery is of no consequence to a composer who has no wish to emulate Wagner by writing symphonic music for the stage. It is true that Rimsky - Korsakov constantly reiterated in the prefaces to his later operas that he 'regarded an opera as first and foremost a *musical* work'. But the course of the story provided him with a ready-made shape, a skeleton to be covered with the flesh of his music. And he usually managed to do the covering very delightfully.

'Opera', Rimsky-Korsakov once remarked to Yastrebtsev, 'is essentially a false artistic genre, but alluring in its spaciousness and its endless variety of forms'. He certainly made the most of that 'endless variety' and one might almost claim that his work summarizes the whole of Russian opera. *The Maid of Pskov* is a less virile, less realistic counterpart of *Boris*, *Mozart and Salieri* obviously a companion-piece to *The Stone Guest*. *Sadko* and *Kitezh* belong, each in its way, to the world of *Prince Igor*. *May Night* and *Snow Maiden* are purely lyrical in Glinka's vein. And though he never wrote anything quite as fine as *Boris* or *Igor*, Korsakov must be granted the quite peculiar power of evoking a fantastic world entirely his own, half-real, half-supernatural, a world as limited, as distinctive and as delightful as the world of the Grimms' fairy-tales or as Alice's Wonderland. It is a world in which the commonplace and matter-of-fact are inextricably confused with the fantastic, naïveté with sophistication, the romantic with the humorous, and beauty with absurdity. He was not its inventor, of course; he owed it in the first place to Pushkin and Gogol. But he gave it a queer touch of his own, linking it with Slavonic antiquity and hinting at pantheistic symbolism, which makes it peculiarly his. And musically, of course, he reigns in it undisputed. He invented the perfect music for such a fantastic world: music insubstantial when it was matched with unreal things, deliciously lyrical when it touched reality, in both cases coloured from the most superb palette musician has ever held.

That he achieved anything higher or deeper than this, Rimsky-Korsakov himself would have been the first to deny. (Though he must have taken himself more seriously than we can as a genuinely *dramatic* composer.) Fully conscious of his own ability, Rimsky-Korsakov—with characteristically cool candour—never made any secret of the fact that he knew his limitations. He was seriously annoyed when people spoke of him as 'a genius'. He knew that he had marvellous talents, but he knew that 'genius' was another matter altogether. 'Don't you think that you value me far too high?' he once said to Yastrebtsev. 'Study Liszt and Balakirev more closely and you'll see that a great deal in me is—*not* me'. Again, later in the course of the same conversation: 'I repeat—by no means from modesty—you overvalue me'. But he was dealing with a hero-worshipper. There is little fear of his being overvalued by people who know him only by a handful of orchestral pieces—and perhaps the 'Hindu Song' from *Sadko*.

BIBLIOGRAPHY

THE main source-book is, of course, Rimsky-Korsakov's own *Letopis moey Muzikalnoy Zhizni*, originally published in 1909, though the first nearly full unexpurgated and corrected edition was the third, edited by his son Andrey and published in 1928. English translations by Judah A. Joffe of the original edition and the fuller text appeared in 1923 and 1942 respectively. This is valuably supplemented by Andrey Rimsky-Korsakov's *N. A. Rimsky-Korsakov: Zhizn i Tvorchestvo* in five volumes, of which the first appeared in 1933. Rimsky-Korsakov was 'Boswellized' by V. V. Yastrebtsev, but unfortunately only the first two volumes of *Moi Vospominaniya o N. A. Rimskom-Korsakove* have ever been published (Moscow, 1917). Korsakov's correspondence with V. V. Stassov was published in *Russkaya Misl* (1910), that with Balakirev in the *Muzikalny Sovremennik* (1915–17), and that with Lyadov in the *Muzikalny Sovremennik* (1915–16). A very full bibliography of books and articles on Rimsky-Korsakov in the Russian language was printed in *Sovetskaya Muzika* for May 1933.

Of the foreign books on Rimsky-Korsakov, by far the solidest is N. van Gilse van der Pals' *N. A. Rimsky-Korssakow: Opernschaffen* (Leipzig, 1929) which analyses all the operas in great detail. Markevitch's *Rimsky-Korsakov* (Paris, 1935) is interesting mainly for its illustrations. My own *Studies in Russian Music* and *On Russian Music* (William Reeves, 1935 and 1939) contain a number of essays on various aspects of Rimsky-Korsakov's work; a study of his songs appeared in the *Monthly Musical Record* for March 1944.

RIMSKY-KORSAKOV'S COMPOSITIONS

OPERAS

None. *The Maid of Pskov* (1868–72; revised and re-orchestrated 1877[1]; third version 1891–92; additional aria in Act III, 1898).

None. *Mlada* (choruses for Act II, and the first part of Act III of an opera-ballet in collaboration with Cui, Mussorgsky, Borodin and Minkus) (1872).

None. *May Night* (1877–79).

None. *Snow Maiden* (1880–81); orchestration revised in the 1890's.

None. *Mlada* (1889–90).

None. *Christmas Eve* (1894–95).

None. *Sadko* (1894–96).

48. *Mozart and Salieri* (1897).

54. *Boyarinya Vera Sheloga* (composed 1877 as Pro-logue to *The Maid of Pskov*; partly rewritten as separate one-act opera, 1898).

None. *The Tsar's Bride* (1898; additional aria in Act III, 1899).

None. *The Tale of Tsar Saltan, of his son the famous and mighty hero Prince Gvidon Saltanovich and of the beautiful Swan Princess* (1899–1900).

None. *Servilia* (1900–1901).

None. *Kashchey the Immortal* (1901–1902; end re-written 1906).

None. *Pan Voevoda* (1902–1903).

None. *The Legend of the Invisible City of Kitezh and the Virgin Fevroniya* (1903–1905).

[1] See also under Orchestral works.

OPUS NO.

None. *The Golden Cockerel* (1906–1907).

Sketches for an opera on *Stenka Razin* (1906).

Sketches for an operatic 'mystery' on Byron's *Heaven and Earth* (1906), afterwards used by Maximilian Steinberg in his 'dramatic poem' of the same title, Op. 12 (1918).

ORCHESTRAL WORKS

1. Symphony No. 1 in E flat minor (1861–65; revised and reorchestrated, in E minor, 1884).

28. *Overture on Russian Themes* (1866; revised and reorchestrated 1879–80).

6. *Fantasia on Serbian Themes* (1867; reorchestrated 1888).

5 (originally 7). *Episode from the legend of Sadko* (1867; revised and re-styled 'Musical picture, *Sadko*' 1869 [1]; third version—published as 'second'—1892).

9. Symphony No. 2 (*Antar*) (1868; revised and reorchestrated 1875; again revised and reorchestrated 1897; re-styled 'symphonic suite,' 1903).

32. Symphony No. 3 in C (scherzo 1866; trio 1872; the rest 1873; revised and re-orchestrated 1885–86).

None. Overture and Entr'actes for Mey's drama *The Maid of Pskov* (1877; reorchestrated 1882).[2]

31. *Sinfonietta on Russian Themes* (based on first three movements of a string quartet written in 1879; revised and orchestrated 1880–84).

29. *Legend* (originally entitled *Baba-Yaga*) (1879–80).

---

[1] This was the first published version.

[2] The overture (afterwards used as the overture to *Vera Sheloga*) and first two entr'actes were taken bodily from the unpublished second version of the opera; the third and fourth entr'actes were newly composed on material from this second version.

OPUS NO. .

34.   *Spanish Capriccio* [1] (1887).

35.   Symphonic suite, *Sheherazade* (1888).

36.   *Easter Festival (Overture on liturgical themes)* (1888).

57.   *Musical Pictures to ' The Tale of Tsar Saltan'* (suite from the opera) (1899).

59.   Suite from the opera *Pan Voevoda* (1903).

None. Variation 4 (A major) from collaborative *Variations on a Russian Theme* (1903).

61.   Prelude, *On the Tomb* (In Memory of M. P. Belaev) (1904).

62.   *Dubinushka* (folk-song arranged for orchestra, with chorus *ad lib.*, 1905; lengthened 1906).

None. *Night on Mount Triglav* (concert arrangement of Act III of *Mlada*—Korsakov's own *Mlada* of 1890—for orchestra only) (1907).[2]

None. *Greeting* (for Glazunov's jubilee) (1907).

None. *Neapolitan · Song* (arrangement of *Funiculi, funicula*) (1907).

None. *Introduction and Wedding March* from *The Golden Cockerel* (concert arrangement for orchestra only) (1907).

Sketches for a Symphony in B minor (1867), the third movement (Rondo scherzando) of a Fourth Symphony (1884), a *Little Russian Fantasia* on Ukrainian themes (1887), and a symphonic poem on Pushkin's *Tale of the Fisherman and the Fish* (1907).

WORKS FOR SOLO INSTRUMENT WITH ORCHESTRA OR MILITARY BAND

None. Variations on Glinka's song, *Chto krasotka molodaya,* for oboe and military band (1878).

---

[1] Based on a projected *Fantasia on Spanish Themes* for violin and orchestra.

[2] Rimsky-Korsakov also made concert suites both from *Mlada* and from *Christmas Eve.*

OPUS NO.

None. Concerto for trombone and military band (1878?).

None. *Concertstück* in E flat for clarinet and military band (1878).

30. Concerto in C sharp minor for piano and orchestra (1882–83).

33. *Fantasia on Russian ·Themes*, for violin and orchestra (1886).

None. *Souvenir de trois hants polonais*, for violin and orchestra (1888–93).[1]

CHAMBER MUSIC

12. String Quartet in F (1875).

None. String Sextet in A (1876).

None. Quintet in B flat for piano, flute, clarinet horn and bassoon (1876).

None. *String Quartet on Russian Themes* (1879).[2]

None. First movement of collaborative *Quartet on the theme B-la-F* (1886).

None. Finale (*Khorovod*) of the collaborative *Name-Day Quartet* (*Jour de Fête*) (1887).

None. String Quartet in G (1897).

None. Trio in C minor for piano, violin and 'cello (1897).

None. Allegro in B flat, for string quartet, for the album *Les Vendredis*.

None. Variation 4 (G major) from collaborative *Variations on a Russian Theme*, for string quartet (1899).

37. *Serenade* for 'cello and piano (1903).

[1] The Polish themes of this unpublished work were afterwards used in the opera *Pan Voevoda*.

[2] Three movements were orchestrated as the Sinfonietta, Op. 31; see also under Piano music.

PIANO WORKS

OPUS NO.

None. Overture (unfinished) (1855).

None. Allegro in D minor (1859–60).

None. Variations on a Russian theme (1859–60).

None. Nocturne in D minor (1860).

None. Funeral March in D minor (1860).

None. Scherzo in C minor, for piano duet (1860).

15. Three Pieces (Valse, Romance and Fugue) (1875).

17. Six Fugues (1875).

10. Six Variations on the theme B-A-C-H (Valse, Intermezzo, Scherzo, Nocturne, Prelude and Fugue) (1878).

11. Four Pieces (Impromptu, Novellette, Scherzino and Etude) (1878).

None. Variations 1, 2, 6, 11, 12, 13, 16 and 19 [1] for the collaborative *Paraphrases* (1879).

None. *In Church*, for piano duet (1879).[2]

None. Figure Six, from collaborative *Joke-Quadrille* (1885).

38. Prelude-Impromptu and Mazurka, for the Bessel *Jubilee Album* (1894).

None. Fugal Intermezzo for piano duet (intended for the opera *Mozart and Salieri*) (1897).

None. Variation 1 (A major) from collaborative *Variations on a Russian Theme*, for piano (1900).

[1] Other, unpublished, variations are mentioned by Rimsky-Korsakov in his autobiography: a sonatina, the chorale *Ein feste Burg*, a '*recitative alla J. S. Bach*,' etc.

[2] Originally *In the Monastery*, the finale of the String Quartet on Russian Themes.

CHORAL WORKS

13.   Two 3-part Choruses for female voices *a capella* (1875).

14.   *Four Variations and Fughetta on a Russian Folk-Song*, for 4-part female chorus, with harmonium or piano *ad lib.* (1875).

16.   Six *a capella* Choruses (various combinations) (1875–76).

18.   Two Choruses (mixed voices) (1876).

23.   Four 3-part Choruses for male voices *a capella* (1876).

20.   *Alexey the Man of God*, folk-song arranged for chorus and orchestra (1877).

19.   *Fifteen Russian Folk-Songs* arranged for chorus *a capella* (five for female, five for male and five for mixed voices) (1879).

21.   *Slava*, folk-song arranged for chorus and orchestra (1876–80).

None. *We praise Thee, O God,* Greek chant arranged for double chorus (1883).

22.   Liturgical Music (eight settings from the Liturgy of St. John Chrysostom) (1883).

22b.   Liturgical Music (arrangements of traditional chants) (1884).

44.   *Switezianka*, cantata for soprano and tenor soli, chorus and orchestra [1] (1897).

58.   *Song of Oleg the Wise*, for tenor and bass soli, male chorus and orchestra (1899).

60.   *From Homer*, prelude-cantata for soprano, mezzo and contralto soli, female chorus and orchestra.

---

[1] Incorporating a modified version of the solo song of the same title, Op. 7, No. 3.

VOCAL DUETS, TRIOS, ETC.

OPUS NO.

None. *The Butterfly*, duet with piano accompaniment (1855).

47.   Two Duets with piano accompaniment (1897; orchestrated 1905).

52.   Two Duets with piano accompaniment (1897–98; No. 1 rearranged as vocal trio with orchestral accompaniment, as Op. 52*b*, 1905).

53.   *Dragon-Flies*, trio for female voices with piano or orchestra, and female chorus *ad lib.* (1897).

SONGS

None. *Vikhodi ko mne, Signora* (1861).

None. *V krovi gorit* (1865).

2.   Four Songs (1865–66).

3.   Four Songs (1886; No. 1 orchestrated 1888).

4.   Four Songs (1866).

7 (originally 5). Four Songs (1867).

8.   Six Songs (1868–70).

25.   Two Songs (1870 and 1877).

26.   Four Songs (1882).

27.   Four Songs (1883),

39.   Four Songs (1897).

40.   Four Songs (1897).

41.   Four Songs (1897).

42.   Four Songs (1897).

43.   *In Spring* (four songs) (1897).

45.   *To the Poet* (five songs) (Nos. 1–4, 1897; No. 5, 1899).

46.   *By the Sea* (five songs (1897).

OPUS NO.

49. Two Ariosos for bass (1897 [1]; No. 2 orchestrated 1899, No. 1, 1906).

50. Four Songs (1897–98).

51. Five Songs (1897).

55. Four Songs for tenor (1897–98).

56. Two Songs for soprano (No. 1 orchestrated 1905, No. 2, 1906).

FOLK-SONG COLLECTIONS

None. *Forty Folk-Songs*, collected by T. I. Filippov and harmonized by Rimsky-Korsakov (1875).

24. *Collection of Russian Folk-Songs* (1875–76).

LITERARY WORKS

Textbook of Harmony (1884).

Record of my Musical Life (1876–1906).

Principles of Orchestration (1896–1908).

Collected Articles and Notes on Music (published 1911).

WORK ON COMPOSITIONS BY COLLEAGUES AND OTHERS

Schubert's *March for the Coronation of Nicholas I*, orchestrated (1868).

First number of Cui's opera *William Ratcliffe*, orchestrated (1868).

Dargomïzhsky's opera *The Stone Guest*, orchestrated (1869; first scene reorchestrated about 1900, the remainder reorchestrated and certain passages rewritten, 1902).

Chorus of Maidens from Dargomïzhsky's opera *Rogdana*, orchestrated (1873?).

[1] The first sketch of No. 1, *The Upas-Tree*, dates from 1882.

Trio (second version) of Mussorgsky's *Destruction of Sennacherib*, orchestrated (1874; Rimsky-Korsakov afterwards orchestrated the whole work with the original trio).

Seven numbers from Handel's *Samson*, orchestrated (1875–76).

Glinka's *Life for the Tsar* and *Ruslan and Lyudmila* edited (with Balakirev and Lyadov) (1878–81); Glinka's complete works edited (with Glazunov) (1907).

Final chorus of Borodin's *Prince Igor*, orchestrated (1879); Prologue and Scene 1 of Act I revised (1885); whole opera completed and orchestrated (with Glazunov) (1887–88).[1]

Persian Dances from Mussorgsky's *Khovanshchina*, edited and orchestrated (1879); whole opera rewritten, completed and orchestrated (1881–83).

Miscellaneous orchestral and choral works, songs, etc., by Mussorgsky, edited and in some cases reorchestrated (1881–83).

Dream intermezzo from Mussorgsky's opera *Sorochintsy Fair* rewritten and re-scored for orchestra only, as *Night on the Bare Mountain* (1886).

Excerpts from Glinka's operas, arranged for string orchestra (1884).

Nocturne from Borodin's Second String Quartet, arranged for solo violin and orchestra (1887).

Polonaise from Mussorgsky's *Boris Godunov*, reorchestrated (1888); Coronation Scene reorchestrated (1892); whole opera, with severe cuts, rewritten and reorchestrated (1892–96); cuts restored in rewritten and reorchestrated form (1906); two additional passages composed for the Coronation Scene at Dyagilev's request for the Paris production (1907).

[1] For a detailed account of Rimsky-Korsakov's and Glazunov's editorial work on *Prince Igor* see the present writer's book *On Russian Music* (William Reeves, 1939).

Borodin's Finale to Act IV of the collaborative *Mlada*, orchestrated (1890).

Borodin's song *The Sleeping Princess*, orchestrated (1897).

Borodin's song *The Sea*, orchestrated (1906).

Mussorgsky's opera-fragment *The Marriage* revised and partly orchestrated (1906).

Mussorgsky's songs *Hopak*, *Gathering Mushrooms* and *Peasant Lullaby* orchestrated (1906).

'Free musical rendering' of Mussorgsky's song *With Nurse* (1908).

Mussorgsky's songs *Night* and *The Field-Marshal*, and part of *Serenade* (from *Songs and Dances of Death*) orchestrated (1908).

TRANSCRIPTIONS FOR MILITARY BAND (1873–83)

Coronation March from *Le Prophète*.

Isabella's Aria from *Robert le Diable* (solo clarinet and military band).

Conspiracy Scene from *Les Huguenots*.

Berlioz's version of Meyer's *Moroccan March*.

Schubert's March in B minor.

Prelude to *Lohengrin*.

Nocturne and Wedding March from Mendelssohn's *Midsummer Night's Dream* music.

Overture to *Egmont*.

Music for the stage-band in Glinka's *Ruslan and Lyudmila* (1878).